HOW
2 GERBILS
20 GOLDFISH
200 GAMES
2000 BOOKS AND I
TAUGHT THEM
HOW TO READ

HOW
2 GERBILS
20 GOLDFISH
200 GAMES
2000 BOOKS AND I
TAUGHT THEM
HOW TO READ

by STEVEN DANIELS

THE WESTMINSTER PRESS
Philadelphia

ISBN 0-664-20904-1 (cloth)
ISBN 0-664-24913-2 (paper)

LIBRARY OF CONGRESS CATALOG CARD NO. 78-141992

PUBLISHED BY THE WESTMINSTER PRESS®
PHILADELPHIA, PENNSYLVANIA

PRINTED IN THE UNITED STATES OF AMERICA

For Connie L. ("Mom") Stern,
who helped me build the car
and
For Leon N. ("Pops") Stern,
who helped me pave the road

CONTENTS

ACKNOWLEDGMENTS

AT HOME
    My wife, Patrice, for a smile, a sigh, and a bounce.
    My sister, Lynn, for excitement.
    Malcolm Rabbit, who devoured the manuscript.

AT THE TYPEWRITER
    My Mother, for the chicken soup of the mind.
    Fred, an excellent teacher of the physically absent.
    Chuck, who reads the lines as well as between them.
    David, for instructions in letting it be.
    Brett and Leo, for a good "hourse" laugh.
    Cumbres, where it is easier to create.

AT THE SCHOOL
    Vera Showers, Willie Starks, Vernetta Lancaster, and
        all their friends, for teaching me.
    Samuel Staff, for having the courage to take risks.
    Dave Friedman, my favorite roster man.

Sue, Alex, Max, Lawyer, Marion, Vivian, Stuart, Helen, Barbara, Elliott, and Paul, for making it a good place to be.

OTHERS

The Suids, and *About Education: The Magazine of the Philadelphia Schools,* for a most important introduction, for permission to reprint from articles of mine, and for "The Little Piece of Coal," by Jackie Lewis.

Mary Steyn, and *The Reader's Digest,* for encouragement, and for permission to reprint from my article, "My Wondrous Education as a Ghetto Teacher."

Grove Press, Inc., for permission to quote from *The Autobiography of Malcolm X,* copyright © 1964 by Alex Haley and Malcolm X, copyright © 1965 by Alex Haley and Betty Shabazz.

Dædalus, Journal of the American Academy of Arts and Sciences, Boston, Massachusetts, for permission to quote from John R. Seeley's "Remaking the Urban Scene," Vol. 97, No. 4, Fall, 1968.

Being and Nothingness, by Jean-Paul Sartre, by permission of Philosophical Library, Inc., translated by Hazel Barnes, copyright © 1956, Philosophical Library, Inc.

PREFACE

Many of the stories and incidents that I describe in the following pages have been "condensed" out of their original order.

The school that I teach in is predominantly black. But when I mention "these children," I am referring to all students who are not making the kind of academic progress they could. Poverty and inferior instruction cut across racial lines.

Three or four of the anecdotes and characters I talk about are based on the experiences of friends who teach in schools similar to mine. The rest, of course, come from my own experiences.

PREFACE

INTRODUCTION: "THIS MUST BE THE PLACE . . ."

You arrive at The Place at about the same time every day—how many years has it been now? You wait, along with The Others, in a small area . . . until The Assistant to one of The Big Ones comes to get you. You wait in the winter snow, you wait in the summer heat, but always you must wait for The Assistant. Finally, he comes, and you and The Others are shunted into the squat, gray edifice.

As you are marched upward, you are reminded of the strangeness of The Place. The Place has nonmoving stairs which have the highly specialized capacity to go only up or down. But not both.

At the landing you turn and walk down a passageway which, by some long-forgotten edict, has just one side. You stop at your numerically personalized metallic storage space. There you gather together the essentials necessary for negotiating the next period of time. Then, follow a subconsciously engraved route to your first Cubicle. You sit. Under no circumstances are you to arise. Not even for the entry into The Cubicle of The Big One No. 1.

He enters slowly and lets his eyes meander to where you and The Others sit. His ears wander in between your seats. You and The Others remain motionless. The Big Ones are all capable of becoming enraged at even the slightest sound. Satisfied, Big One No. 1 nods his head. He turns and places himself behind his protective encasement. Then, and only then, does Big One No. 1 begin to speak. His voice is raspy; it grates. But you listen anyway: maybe today you will be able to crack the code he uses.

Some of his language is so familiar. Some of the words sound like the ones you use. The inflections and patterns are similar to those of your own tongue. Big One No. 1 speaks them as if there were something he wanted very much to tell you. But you cannot understand The Big Ones at all.

Next, as has become his habit, he turns away from his barrier and with the extension of his right arm begins to scratch lines of white images on a black background. Long ago you learned that this is the signal for you and The Others to reproduce carefully those white images from the black background with your own black images on a white background.

Suddenly, Big One No. 1 wheels around! He has heard one of The Others make a noise! Slowly, with reverberating footsteps, he approaches that Other. With a well-practiced stroke he crashes the extension of his left arm onto Other's backside. The Other, although in great pain, knows better than to make another sound. Doing so would invite the severest of penalties. Other would not be permitted entry to The Place for a long time. And Other is not allowed anywhere else.

The incident over, you turn your attention back to the black background. You continue as meticulously as before to carbon The Big One's hieroglyphics. A low, wheezing tone vibrates from the box on the wall. Now you must leave the first Cubicle . . . and enter the second.

Big One No. 2 appears. No. 2's actions closely resemble those of No. 1. His language, arm extensions, and encasements are the same. Big One No. 1 and Big One No. 2 differ in only minor ways. No. 2, for instance, does not make the white marks on the black. Instead, he gives each of The Others a large pile of bound paper. Each sheet has the same kind of funny lines and spaces that No. 1 put on the background. Big One No. 2 speaks, then returns to his barrier. Not sure of what to do, and very bored, you begin to draw your own lines on the sheets.

The low wheeze interrupts you. You and The Others must now proceed to the third Cubicle and Big One No. 3. You begin walking down the one-sided passageway. . . .

"I really wish I could teach these slum kids, but frankly it's an impossible job. The real problem isn't so much teaching them; it's trying to get them disciplined enough to be in a position to learn anything. These kids just don't know what it is to keep quiet for more than five seconds at a time, and when I'm trying to teach thirty or thirty-five of them at once, five seconds simply won't do. It's not even keeping them quiet. It gets down to things as elementary as getting them to sit still. They keep fidgeting around, and then the fidgeting turns into a fight, and then you end up acting like a warden in a state pen. It's true what they say: Slum school teachers end up as not-too-well-paid baby-sitters.

"I'm not quite sure why they act that way. Maybe some of it's because they can't read. Endless months of trying to handle eighth-grade students who can't understand even a grade-school English text. It's not bad enough they can't read the books. What's worse is that they continually destroy them.

"I wonder why their parents don't teach them some respect for property? Or, for that matter, why their parents let them come to school smelling that way? And wearing the most awful-looking rags? Their parents just must not care. Why, the last Parent-Teacher meeting we had during Open School Week, only fifteen parents showed up. That's out of 1500 kids that are enrolled in my school. Ninety-nine percent of the parents just don't care.

"All that wouldn't be so bad if I could only teach these kids something. I keep telling them and telling them that the signs on the subway and the buses (which they can't read) are true, that you can't get a good job without a good education. But somehow these kids don't seem to want to listen.

"I know the lessons I prepare are good, and that they're important, but the kids just don't understand. Take a look at this world map. [See page opposite]. From an open

WORLD MAP (outline)

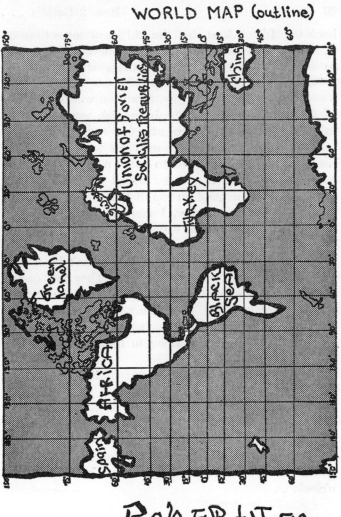

ROBERT+JEN

book too. It's obvious that the kid spent some time on it, shading it in just right. Can you believe it? According to him, we're all living in Sub-Sahara Africa!

"But then what can you expect? Look at the English lesson I gave them yesterday. I put ten words, only ten of them, on the board. Simple enough words—I'm up to the 'C's'—words like 'catastrophe' and 'compromise,' and I told the kids to look up each word in the dictionary, define it, and then to write it in a sentence. I even warned them that there would be a test on the same words today. And on top of that we went over all the words in class. Today, I marked the papers. Two kids passed. And passing's only 60 percent. Two kids out of thirty.

"Even their reading and writing wouldn't be so bad if they could learn to speak English. They just cannot speak the language. I wouldn't have believed it if I hadn't heard it myself. They can't even say words like 'ridiculous' and 'flammable,' words they're supposed to know. How can you get along in today's world if you can't speak English?

"I don't really know which part of it is worse. The discipline problems get so bad that I have to take a ruler to some kids, and I don't enjoy that. But then these kids won't respond to anything but force—half the time they act like animals. The teaching, well, to be honest, I can't say that I teach at all. But the job has its compensations. It's secure, long vacations, I'm out by three o'clock. . . ."

An unlikely juxtaposition of two extremes? Not one bit. For the slum child, school is at best an awkward-feeling fantasy, a never-ending movement from Cubicle to Cubicle, from Big One to Big One. Surprisingly, some of these students don't develop an antagonistic feeling toward the entire routine. They simply remain bewildered. Most, however, finally agree with all the teachers who called them "ignorant failures."

The teacher who described the hardships of his work is not yet the hardened, child-hating type found in Jonathan Kozol's *Death at an Early Age*. He uses the ruler to keep order so that he can try to teach. And he is sincere in his efforts. By the end of his second or third year, though, the ruler has become a means of self-defense, and he masks his own bitter failure with indifference and/or a preoccupation with petty rules and regulations.

The results of this void, for it has passed far beyond the stage of being one of the presently popular "gaps," are hopelessly walking the streets looking for a job. Those without hope wait in line for a check. And those whom the educational system has completely warped are waiting around the corner with a knife, or perhaps a gun.

I know. I've seen some of the children whom I've failed to reach spend their summer looting. I've crossed names out of my classroom roll book after reading the headline: "Gang Killings in Philadelphia Claim Another Victim."

But I've seen much more of the other side. I've watched children I teach improve in reading ability from the third-grade level to the seventh-grade level in ten months. I've worked with students who could not write their name—not a cliché where I work—and have received their first shakily scrawled essay. I've seen long lines of school-hating students eagerly look forward to staying after three o'clock for an hour, two hours, as long as I would let them.

Over the past four years I have worked out a few

theories that may help explain what goes wrong in most
ghetto classrooms. More important, I have developed
several methods, techniques, and general practices for
rectifying this almost-static situation. Many of them
are new and are not usual classroom procedure. Others
are simply the application of new logic to an old situation. They have worked for me, and they have worked
for those with whom I've shared them. They cannot be,
of course, the ultimate solution to all the ills of urban
education. But they are, I hope, the first steps in a long
overdue journey.

My hypothetical teacher will probably look up from the
page now and mutter, ". . . impossible to educate these
kids. Just to begin with, what about discipline. . . ."
And so that's the place to start.

1

"WHO'S ON FIRST?"

Walking through the halls of public schools, I hear the muted screams of teachers trying to keep their classes quiet. I question why their students are being told to "shut up!" Perhaps these teachers will discover, as I did, that not much can be learned in an atmosphere that is constricted with silence.

Very few children, especially in the early grades, have the mental ability to suppress their natural physical energy. Nor should they. Human interaction on almost any level requires some degree of noise, and most education is a result of human interaction, not of attending classroom lectures. In addition, many urban children have great difficulty either with self-expression or with the actual psychomotor skills associated with physically talking. Keeping these students quiet is detrimental.

Although discipline may be a prerequisite to classroom

learning, it shouldn't be assumed that it's synonymous with silence. Nor does discipline mean sitting in assigned seats in assigned rows, begging to be allowed to go to the bathroom, or anything similar. Rather, discipline should be defined as the ability to obtain order in the room when, for whatever reason, it is needed.

The urban school teacher, in trying to establish order, or classroom control, faces problems that his suburban or private school counterpart doesn't. Probably the most important difference between the two is that the suburban teacher can rely upon what I call "Control from Without," whereas the ghetto teacher must count almost solely on "Control from Within."

Outside the ghetto, the teacher is only one among several other voices of authority. If one of his students becomes a discipline problem, the suburban teacher knows that he has many recourses. First, the child may be sent to other school authorities who will try to curb his rebelliousness. Failing this, the student's parents will be called to school. Suburban parents, generally concerned for their children's welfare, will almost always respond to the school's request for their cooperation. In cases where this doesn't produce a change in the student's behavior, still further action can be taken. In a private school, the student will be asked to leave. In a public school, he will most likely be sent to a disciplinary class or room (a room where disruptive children are forced to sit quietly, usually supervised by a teacher or a nonteaching assistant).

Even all these steps don't convey the full significance of Control from Without. Behind the immediate authority there rests a social system that demands the proper credentials for admission to "the good life": the grades and recommendations that will assure the student's admission to college. Given this array of external support, even the weakest teacher will be able to maintain control of his class.

In an urban school, on the other hand, the teacher is the ultimate social force in the classroom. Sending a difficult child to school authorities rarely results in positive action. White administrators in predominantly black schools are often afraid of the reprisals from militant parents that might follow the suspension of a student. In ghetto schools where race is not a factor there is often no disciplinary room or class available—for lack of funds or space or both. Since the child is already at the bottom of the academic scale, he cannot be threatened with expulsion to another school. Special schools, like the 600's in New York City, and reformatories, for severe cases, are so overcrowded that it's almost impossible to have a child admitted. I found this out the hard way during my first year of teaching.

Marsha Brown, a severely disturbed thirteen-year-old, stabbed me in the arm with her pencil, leaving what turned out to be a permanent scar. Despite her reputation for assaulting other teachers, it took over three months to get her transferred to a disciplinary girls school. During that period she continued to sit—rather ominously—in my class, a perfect example to my other students of lack of Control from Without.

As in the suburbs, it's possible to request that a child's parents come to school. For a variety of reasons, this frequently fails (see Chapter 8). Urban parents don't provide a teacher the control leverage given by suburban parents.

Further, if we look at the entire structure from the urban child's viewpoint, we find that the social forces that predominate in the suburban "Other America" have no meaning. The great majority of ghetto youth are not preoccupied with college admissions. They have even less fear of losing their opportunity to lead "the good life," for while they may vaguely hope for it, they have no concrete experience of it. For the ghetto student, then, "when you got nothin', you got nothin' to lose."

The urban teacher, to initiate and maintain Control from Within must do two things. To maintain it, he must create "something to lose." The curriculum he establishes must be so exciting that there is no need for disciplinary measures. To initiate it, he must fill the "leadership void" at the beginning of the year.

The natural apprehensiveness of both the teacher and the student when school starts in September creates, however temporarily, a void in leadership. Neither party is entirely sure of itself. This is especially true of new teachers. How the teacher reacts to student challenges during that first week eventually determines who is leading whom. In a suburban or private school, student tests of the teacher's ability to lead are largely pro forma: both know that the teacher will prevail. In a ghetto school, however, students seriously and validly question whether the teacher will assume the leadership. It wouldn't be slanderous to claim that some ghetto students collect teacher resignations as coin collectors search for Indian-head pennies. These children know from experience, and the turnover rate of urban school teachers confirm, that they can win the war of limits and endurance.

It's been said that when a new ghetto teacher walks into his classroom on the first day of school everybody turns the other way—including God. I'm still grateful that nobody was watching me the first day.

On that morning I distributed paper and pencils to my seventh-grade students and gave them a quiz to determine their knowledge of current events. In the middle of the fifth question the first paper airplane sallied forth.

"Who threw that paper airplane?"
Silence.
"I said, 'Who threw that paper airplane?'"
Silence.
"Never mind. We'll continue."

By the end of the test I could have gone into the airline business.

On the second day a pencil from the back of the room landed near my desk. Simultaneously a voice from the rear screamed,

"Geez, man, I dropped my pencil."
"Well, then, come and get it."

Which was all the provocation Calvin Gordon needed to take a ten-minute circus strut to the front of the room, laboriously stoop to retrieve his pencil, and apologize ever so sincerely. He proceeded to introduce himself to half a dozen of his new classmates on the way back

to his seat. (No need to be too harsh with him, it's only
the second day, I thought.)

The third day was one of general chaos: student
friendships were budding.

> (To the left side of the room): "Will you
> kindly keep quiet so that we may continue?"
>
> Silence on the left side.
>
> (To the right side of the room): "Please have
> the courtesy to keep your mouths closed."
>
> Silence on the right side.
>
> (Back to the left side): "Will you please
> shut up?"

By the end of the week my students knew one another
well enough to have disagreements that resulted in classroom fistfights.

> (Slamming a ruler on the desk): "Now sit
> down and shut up!"
>
> (On the second bounce the ruler breaks):
> "Now that's just about enough out of you two!
> Sit down immediately!"

By the end of the month the entire situation was
helpless and hopeless. I was hoarse, out over a dozen
rulers, and teaching nothing.

Belatedly, I attempted to gain control of the class. In-
experienced and frustrated, I handled the chaos as best
I could, with an inappropriate choice of familiar disciplinary techniques. I interrupted the next fight by sending the rivals to opposite corners of the room. The fight
continued verbally from one corner to the other. I sent
behavior problems to the office. Fifteen minutes later they

were back in the room causing further disorder. Other students were told to "Go home and write two hundred times: 'I will keep quiet in Room 407.'" They responded by shrugging their shoulders and turning in blank pieces of paper. Eventually, I acknowledged that these and similar approaches were senseless and a waste of time. I dropped them.

As the months grated on, the objects flying in my classroom increased in volume and weight—from September planes to April chairs. Early in May, at the end of a particularly trying class, one brave young girl came up to me and whispered softly but clearly, "Mr. Daniels, they has been makin' a ass-hole whipe outa you."

In the beginning of June, I gave up altogether. I turned on the government-donated television and the children spent the last four weeks of school watching *Dennis the Menace* (which struck me as being a not inappropriate choice). What had been obvious to my students from the first few days was now clear to me. By reacting to them instead of initiating action myself, I had failed to provide decisive leadership.

Returning to that first day: those students who attempt to usurp the teacher's authority are trying to establish their own rep—reputation and following. If the teacher can cope with these first challengers, he will win two victories. First, he will demonstrate to them the seriousness of his intention to lead. Second, the class as a whole will understand his intent. In addition, there is a probable dividend. The challenging students will most likely fulfill their desire to become influential members of the class, and for the rest of the year they will remind their

friends that it's "dangerous to mess with Mr. —————."
If this sounds like a mental battlefield, it has not been
misrepresented. But the teacher has one large tactical
advantage. His new students do not know (or remember,
as the case may be) one another well enough either to
present a united front of misbehavior or to feel comfortable supporting the one or two who will try to in-
stigate it. If the teacher doesn't utilize this chance to
assert his authority, the children soon will.

During my second year (and ever since) I provided
leadership from the outset. Ten minutes after the start
of the first class the perennial pencil landed near my
desk. The cry from the back of the room approximated
its annual predecessors:

> "Oops, the pencil slipped outa my hand."
> (Returning the pencil to him, calmly): "It is
> against the rules of my room to throw things.
> The next person who breaks one of my rules
> will be in deep trouble."

Inevitably, another pencil slips to the front of the room.

> (Returning the pencil, still calm): "It's too
> bad that you have to find out so early in the
> year that I mean exactly what I say. What time
> will your mother be home tonight?"
> (Somewhat surprised): "My mom gets home
> from work at six."
> "Tell her to expect me."
> Tense silence fills the room.

In the child's eyes I had just threatened to jail him

for jaywalking. Very rarely does a teacher walk at night through the slums of North Philadelphia for any reason— and hardly for something as trivial as a slipped pencil on the first day of school. The class was stunned. It was clear that they didn't believe that I would follow through. On the other hand, just in case I would, further challenges to my leadership were momentarily suspended.

By the end of my fifth and last class I had a list of twelve parents, aunts, uncles, and guardians to see. I saw all of them. To each one I expressed my interest in their child's classroom conduct. Their reactions varied. Two of them spoke to me behind chain-latched doors, three let me in but did not offer me a seat, the others were hospitable—one even invited me to stay for dinner. Without exception they were concerned about their child's conduct. Even the most hostile parents promised their help.

The news of my home visits traveled only slightly faster than a break in the stock market. Every student who walked into my room the next morning knew that my actions were as good as my words.

This is not to say that only such an extreme measure will work. Many of my female teacher friends are understandably hesitant about walking through the ghetto at night. But parental help is as near as the telephone or mailbox. The phone, in fact, has a couple of advantages that a visit doesn't. First, more parents can be reached in a shorter time, and second, a phone call often causes less embarrassment than a personal appearance.

A few words about letters home: they should be personally mailed. Having the office mail a come-to-school-about-your-child form letter encourages a day or two delay while it gets cranked out, and even when it arrives it's impersonal. The other easy way out is to ask a student to take the letter home. This is somewhat akin to requesting that someone cut the rope that holds the guillotine over his own head. In neither case will it be delivered. Instead, a teacher should mail the original home and give a carbon copy to the student before he has that student in class again. That way, though the original may not arrive for a few days, the student knows that his teacher has already acted. A final postscript: send critical letters home in personal-size envelopes, complimentary notes home in business size. The former are harder to pry out of the mailbox than the latter.

Requiring acceptable behavior of the children shouldn't, however, imply harshness. Teachers who use corporal punishment and similar methods often get repaid in kind. They compel the individual students in a class to get closer together and to react against him. Such reaction can be physically painful, as was the case with Maddy Jones. Mrs. Jones, though a math teacher, spends most of her waking moments forcing polite behavior and respect for teachers from her students.

> (Arm raised): "Take that hat off in the building, boy. Get that hat off, you hear?
>
> "Don't slouch when I'm talking to you.
>
> "And spit that gum out! How are you going to get anywhere without manners, huh, boy?
>
> "Hey, you look at me when I'm talking to you, you understand?"

Mrs. Jones, a disciplinarian who makes the classical top sergeant look like the headmaster of a progressive school, is constantly surprised at the amount of foot-scraping and coughing in her classes, and she never forgets to tell new teachers about the year when "those ungrateful kids" bombarded her with eggs, oranges, and apples on the last day of school.

Teachers who demand a great deal from their students should be willing to give in equal proportion. There are four rules in my room. The last one reads: "Act reasonably. When I request order, please stop what you're doing and be quiet." The first three assure each child that at any time he may borrow a pencil, some paper, and up to fifty cents. Rules of this kind almost always result in mutual respect.

The ghetto teacher, then, can obtain control of his classroom by the skilled use of technique. Short of terrorism, however, he can't maintain it that way. Keeping classroom order is primarily the product of a significant and engaging curriculum. In making Control from Within effective, this is what the teacher must "create to lose." In other words, if there's no reason to behave, why behave?

The courses of study in most school systems have a mental orientation: They emphasize the role of the mind in learning. Most children are physically oriented, they express themselves best through action. The teacher, in attempting a conciliation of the curriculum and the student, must consider the "how" of his program as carefully as the "what."

For assorted reasons, one of the best hows is grouping. It permits almost completely individualized instruction, encourages physical freedom, and is effective in main-

taining classroom order and academic progress. A single
disruption in a room where thirty students are doing the
same thing at the same time will interrupt twenty-nine
of them and encourage general mayhem. One isolated incident in a group of five will enable twenty-five students
to continue their work. Grouping will also alleviate many
of the special discipline problems found in the ghetto,
such as children who are mentally retarded or emotion-
ally ill. For unsatisfactory reasons—overcrowding, lack
of proper facilities, no trained personnel, etc.—the teacher
will most likely have one or two retarded or disturbed
students in his class.

Joseph Williams, a retarded youngster, comes to my
room every day, walks directly to his seat, and begins to
mumble audibly to himself. Ronald Hampton, in another
class, has acute feelings of persecution. Left seated with
thirty other students he will periodically stand up and
for no apparent reason scream obscenities. Joseph, because of grouping, doesn't hinder his classmates and I can
work alone with him. Ronald, I found, felt enough at
ease to stop shouting when he sat at my desk. The remainder of the class, working in different parts of the
room, are not concerned, as they might otherwise be,
that a student is sitting in the teacher's chair.

Unfortunately, there is one cause of behavior problems
that even the most exciting curriculum cannot help—
the occasional cases of hunger. A child who has not eaten
breakfast or lunch is apt to be restless. Some parents don't
have, or have mismanaged, the forty cents a day ($72.00
a year) their children need to buy a noon meal, and
school funds for this purpose are usually limited. The
only possible solution is for the teacher to supply either

lunch or some way for the child to earn the money he needs. In my room four erased blackboards, at ten cents a board, provide the needed cash.

To summarize: Continuity of classroom control is the result of a program that has meaning for the student (see the next two chapters). A curriculum that is individualized, that encourages each child to work at his own level and pace, and that accounts for this child's need for physical action, will eventually produce the rarest of scenes: a class that will discipline itself. "Discipline trouble," like the spots of measles, is only the symptom of a deeper problem. Either an individual child is upset, which some personal attention should remedy, the course of study is mentally or physically inadequate, which the teacher can change with some experimentation, or the teacher doesn't really believe himself capable of leading the class.

There is a second kind of discipline that rarely concerns those whose sole objective is to get "them" to "sit *down* and shut *up*." This is the social discipline of living. The importance of learning it is obvious. On a large scale, it prevents the complete breakdown of the social structure. On a personal level it gives this future adult the possibility of a more satisfying life and the chance to advance in his to-be-chosen field.

Disciplined living cannot be formally taught in a classroom. Learning it is usually the result of family training reinforced by personal experience. Many urban children, because of their environment, have not been taught to uphold standards traditionally described as respect for property and fulfillment of responsibility. A feeling for

most of these values will come with the building of the
child's self-esteem (see Chapter 6), but even on a superficial level a teacher can provide the circumstances and
materials conducive to experiencing part of this social
discipline. My students, for instance, had this opportunity
to learn respect for property.

Part of my program involves the use of commercial
games. Each Friday the class is free to play with which-
ever ones they choose, from jigsaw puzzles to board
games. The first Friday, I explained that the games belonged to them and were, therefore, their responsibility.
Like most lectures, this one was ineffective.

At the end of the class the room looked like Macy's
basement at closing time on Christmas Eve. Monopoly
cards were stuffed behind the radiators, dice from a
dozen games were strewn across the floor. I picked up
after them.

Just before they returned on Monday, I re-created the
shambled disorder. Then I surprised them by letting
them play with the games again. The chance to learn
respect for property was given to them in a way they
could understand. Also, the condition of not having
property to respect had been avoided, the games were
theirs.

> "Hey, Mr. Daniels, I can't find Marvin Gar-
> dens."
>
> "I'm sorry, but I don't know where it is."
>
> "Mr. Daniels, I'm missing two Spill and Spell
> dice."
>
> "Try looking on the floor."
>
> "Say, where are the batteries for this game?"
>
> "Who took the crayons out of the box?"

> (And final victory): "Boy, did we leave this
> room in a mess."

At the end of the period, without my having once mentioned responsibility, the games were all neatly stacked in their cabinet. Some students didn't participate in the cleanup, and didn't benefit from the situation. Most, however, did.

Because of this and similar experiences, my students began to feel a pride in accepting responsibility. Toward the middle of the year, becoming even more personally concerned about what they now considered their room, the children asked me if they could sand the holes and profanities out of their desks. By three o'clock on "Sanding Day" the desks hadn't been finished. Some forty students voluntarily stayed after school for two hours to complete the job. I'm sure they got more out of this experience than the only two-tone desks in the school.

In conjunction with creating situations where his students can learn social discipline, a teacher should instruct by example. If the leader doesn't adhere to his own standards, his followers certainly won't. If the sign behind the desk says, No EATING IN CLASS, the person sitting at the desk shouldn't be finishing his morning coffee.

2

"JAM TODAY"

Suppose, if you will, that you're one of the students in my school. Suppose further that it's Friday afternoon, time for your seventh-period English class. After settling down at your desk, you look at the board to find out what you're going to be doing for the next forty-some-odd minutes. As a final conjecture, imagine that your English teacher has left two sets of directions, and that you're free to follow either:

> A. Write down fifteen words that you didn't understand from page 10 of the text that we were reading in class yesterday. Find out the meaning of each word and write it down. Then I will put everybody's words on the board, and the entire class will discuss them.

> B. Find two or three classmates who want to

play a word game with you. Begin the game by placing the fifteen lettered dice in the cup. Spill them out on the floor. Then, in two minutes, make as many different words as you can, using only those letters showing on the top of each die. Instructions for scoring are in each game box. See if you can beat your opponents!

Which would you choose? Most likely, B. Only a masochist, or a child who is too filled with apprehension to let his emotions show in school, would select A.

"Well, Lesson B won't teach you anything," say the majority of teachers, to whom effective education is a necessarily dull process that must somehow be endured. "Any real student knows that Lesson A will be more valuable." Well, will it?

Lesson A is only a slight variation on the theme that is played out in every class, every day, all year—the student selects the words he doesn't understand instead of someone else telling him which words he doesn't understand. The child is probably so disinterested in this type of activity that he doesn't even see the directions on the board. Additionally, there's no such thing as a discussion with thirty people. It's difficult enough to have a decent exchange with only four or five. Finally, unless you're a semanticist, there isn't too much you can discuss about a list of words.

Lesson B is different. It attracts the student's attention because it's a change of pace from the usual trivia. It's an involving activity—the student determines the outcome of the game. To do well at Spill and Spell the child must create words out of constantly shifting groups of letters. To confirm the validity of the words he slaps together in the last few seconds before time runs out, "lyspxyl" and "rotub," he must consult a dictionary. If he wants to figure out his score and see where he stands in comparison with his friends', he must be able to add, subtract, and square numbers. (I have repeatedly watched failing math students, kids who "can't add four and five," learn how to square that same nine and every other number between one and ten in under five minutes.)

In fact, by playing Spill and Spell the student is actually doing all the things that the pedagogues expect of him. He is experiencing "relevant work with numbers," while enjoying a "meaningful relationship with word concepts," and is "highly motivated" in an "individualized program format." Also, he is having fun, as illegitimate as that word sounds in a classroom context.

But what happens to the half of the class who doesn't like word games? For it's foolish to think that there are thirty people in the city who, at any given moment in time, want to do exactly the same thing, and it's blatantly absurd to expect that they are all sitting in one teacher's classroom. Maybe some of the children would like playing The Civil War Game, which would teach them which states were aligned against one another, how the location of those states affected the outcome of the war, why the North couldn't grow crops and the South couldn't produce arms, and it might even give them an introductory knowledge of military strategy.

In my room every Friday is Games Day or Free Day (nobody is forced to play games). Even those students who are habitually late for class show up early on Friday, because games are on a first-come basis. The kids run into the room, grab what they want from the games chest, find two or three friends who also want to play that game, and scatter to different parts of the room. There they continue to throw the dice, turn the cards, move the pieces, exchange the money, and spin the wheel until the bell rings. (A list of the ten most popular games in my room is in Chapter 11.)

If invited—about once in every three periods, I join in one of the games. Otherwise, my role as teacher means that I'm available for finding extra people for a game, replacing old batteries, and very occasionally searching for the lost checker. I don't help my students read the instructions. The room is equipped with games on all levels, from ABC Lotto to Mr. President (a 3M Adult Game), and a child who wants to play a difficult game must read the directions himself. If I help him, he learns only that he doesn't really need to read, and he doesn't learn that there are things worth reading. If he really requires assistance, he can ask another student. The child who told his friend that in order to play the game they would have to "read the destructions" discovered his mistake immediately, and will remember the correction far longer than if it had come from me.

If you ask my students, I spend Fridays either sitting around reading a book or fixing up the room. From my point of view, however, I do the following: I demonstrate to the children what I think of education, that it's enjoyable, and I show what I think of them, that they are trusted to the degree that their teacher doesn't feel it necessary to stand over them.

By keeping out of their way, I also allow many of these children their first real experience as children. For this period anyway they have all the childhood materials they've seen on television, games that I took for granted in my home when I was growing up, but which many of them never had. Tangentially, they are becoming slightly aware of the "good life" that I mentioned in the previous chapter. (Suggestions about raising money to pay for all these games are in Chapter 9.)

Beyond even all of this, however, I am teaching them more by *not* teaching than I could otherwise. While I sit reading my book, thirty individual students are simultaneously learning at least four or five skills and/or attitudes each, something that neither I nor the best teacher could directly accomplish. The most puerile and innocuous board game manufactured (and there are many) will teach *at least* all the following skills:

> Reading—the instructions and the various playing accessories, such as the Real Estate cards in Easy Money.
> The ability to follow directions.
> The ability to speak articulately about a specific subject for at least three minutes.
> Manipulating numbers (for a reason).

Occasionally, children learn skills I didn't know they lacked, such as the hand-eye coordination of the class "Checkers King." Week after week, Marty Sworn beat Brian Watts at checkers. It went on for so long that it had become customary for Brian to come over to me at the end of each period and woefully announce how many times Marty had defeated him—five times, three, six. By the middle of the year, Marty was almost convinced that he was invincible. To remove any doubts that he was "the greatest checkers player in the whole world," he publicly dared me to try to beat him.

The next Friday, surrounded by everyone in the class, Marty and I sat down to do battle. The rules of the game were agreed upon: no backward jumping, but kings could move as many spaces along the diagonals in one turn as they wanted. The rest of the kids crowded closer as Marty made the first move. The game was pretty even until we were both down to four kings. In four moves the game was over. All the kids started screaming, "He cheated, he cheated, Mr. Daniels!" And he had. In all good faith, Marty had skipped the diagonals as he obliterated my men. Starting his move in one row, he ended in another row, taking my piece with him. I screamed out a concession and the kids, disgruntled, wandered back to their own games. Then I asked to watch Marty play Brian. During this match, too, Marty mismoved the kings. Brian didn't seem to notice. I sent them both to the nurse. Two weeks later, both boys wore glasses. From that time on, their games were fairly evenly split.

Games can teach a student attitudes as well as skills. My children learn all those attitudes which come from interacting with a group, such as resolving the frequent disputes without calling on the teacher.

Games present a chance for the students to make their own rules, and to discover the results of changing them. Urban children, almost always confronted by predetermined regulations, rarely have this opportunity. Certainly they didn't get it from me at first. Let me explain.

One Friday, walking through the room, I noticed a group of my brightest students playing Monopoly. I

stopped to watch. After a moment or two, I was sure that
they were misinterpreting the instructions. Another minute and I understood what they were doing wrong.
Normally, Monopoly is played to accumulate property,
the properties bringing in rent from opposing players who
have the misfortune to land on them. Usually, the person
with the most built-up property wins the game, as rents
escalate with the addition of houses and hotels. The
students I was watching were playing some confusing
variation of the game. Instead of buying the property
for the cost price listed on the board, say $150.00, they
purchased it for the rent price listed on the property
card, say $12.00. Another player landing on their property
would have to pay a rent of $150.00, the cost price, in-
stead of the regular $12.00 rent. The kids had confused
other rules, too, but this was the most dramatic. Because
of all their misinterpretations, they finished what is usually an all-day game in a little under half an hour.

I interrupted the start of their next match by giving
them a detailed description of how Monopoly should
be played. The kids, very polite, listened attentively. As
I got up to leave, they all nodded. Then, one of the kids
called me back. He proceeded, very patiently, to explain
that they were indeed aware of how Monopoly was
played and had been for years, but they found that they
never had enough time to finish a complete game in one
class period. Therefore, he said, they revised the rules
so that they could complete at least one game before the
bell rang. Properly rebuked, I returned to my book.

Games are not the only things that the children can
play with on Fridays. The room also has many vocational
materials: typewriters, chemistry and biology sets, a tape

recorder, a mini-printing press, sewing machine, phonograph and records, and a small electric organ. Each of these has an educational value. The story of Mark the Robot serves as an example.

Mark the Robot, named after his creator, was the brainchild of a child whom I gave no credit for brains. One Friday in January he pulled the erector set out of the cabinet. He spent the entire period puttering around, looking at the pieces, examining each nut and bolt. Toward the end of the class, I went over to him and asked if he'd like to see the instruction booklet, which had ideas and directions for building bridges and towers. "Naw, I don't want to look at that old book. I'm gonna build me a robot." Convinced that his would be a fleeting interest, I dropped my suggestion.

Every Friday for the next three months, Mark worked on the erector set. For the first few weeks, I could see no progress, though I admired his persistence. By March, the robot was beginning to take shape. Although I was quite positive that it wouldn't work, I remembered my Monopoly lesson, and kept my mouth shut.

Just before the Easter vacation, Mark came to me and announced that his robot was ready, and did I have a battery? I gave him one, and he hooked it up. Mark the Robot couldn't sing, but it could do just about everything else. The legs moved, the arms moved, and the head twisted from side to side. I gave Mark the erector set as a present, bought a new one for the classroom, and was grateful that I had had the good sense to keep quiet.

Games Day is the high point of my children's week. So high that each Friday I inevitably have to send four or five students who don't belong to me back to their own classrooms, and twice during the last year had to send back entire classes that had sneaked in during the change of periods. (During the 1968–1969 school year my students' Friday attendance exceeded the school's by 12½ percent. On the other four days it was 8 percent higher).

If the kids love the games, most of the faculty remains unimpressed. They consider my classroom little better, or quieter, than an aviary cage at the zoo. At the beginning of one year a colleague, David Rogers, took particular pleasure in repeatedly telling me that I wasted the children's time, and that I taught them nothing. On Fridays, he said, his geography classes sat and drew maps of the United States. I replied that drawing maps was tedious, and that effective education could be fun. After many hours of this kind of argument, we made a bet. I claimed that my students would learn just as much or more about the location of the states by playing games as they would by endlessly drawing and copying.

With the help of a statistician, we set up the following experiment: I would formally teach the geography of the United States to two of my classes. Two of my other classes would be free to play with colorful jigsaw puzzles of the United States for an equal amount of time. We also agreed that my formal teaching had to be as exciting as I could make it, and that I would not in any way help the other group with their puzzles. We chose to do the experiment with only myself and my students to reduce as much as possible the variables of different teachers' personalities.

The classes participating in the experiment were picked randomly. Both groups had thirty students. The academic ability of the Control Group (those to be formally taught), as measured by their reading level, turned out to be 4.9, the Experimental Group's 4.2. Pre- and post-testing were done with a blank outline map of the United States, which the students of both groups had to fill in from memory.

On the pre-test, the Control Group knew 9.2 percent of the states, the Experimental Group 5.4 percent. For one week the Experimental Group played with the puzzles. During that time I "taught" the other group. One day we played Find the State. I picked a student and as he approached the wall map I called out the name of a state. He had five seconds to find it. Another day we played Name the State. I said a letter and the student would point to all those states which started with that letter. The third day we had a State Bee. The other two days the Control Group colored in maps and made lists.

By the first post-test the Control Group's knowledge of the location of the states had increased from 9.2 percent to 27.2 percent, a gain of 295 percent. The Puzzle (Experimental) Group went from 5.4 percent to 13.9 percent, an increase of 260 percent. David and I had stipulated earlier, however, that the true measure of learning was retention. How much would the two groups remember six weeks after the experiment was over?

After the month and a half had elapsed, the final test was given. The Control Group's score went up from 27.2 percent to 28.8 percent. In other words, they remembered more than they had learned. The statistician told us that this kind of "reminiscence" was not unusual. The same pattern was true of the Experimental Group,

whose score rose from 13.9 percent to 17.6 percent. So
the Control Group retained 319 percent of their knowledge, the Experimental Group, 321 percent. Statistically,
the difference was not significant. I concluded that the
"formal" lessons had been too exciting. David disagreed,
but he paid me the quarter. We did agree on one thing,
however, and that was that if a child was going to learn
the same amount anyway, he might as well enjoy it. Sub-
sequently, David began borrowing the puzzles for his
own classes.

How should games and related materials be incorpo-
rated into an educational program? When my classes first
started playing games I thought I'd personally discovered
the Seven Cities of Gold. Move Milton Bradley and
Parker Brothers into the room and move me out, and
that would be that. So, at first, I let my students play
every day. At the end of the first week they grew restless.
After the second week they were bored. A month or so
of trial and error convinced me that one day in five, or
20 percent of classroom time, kept the game interesting,
and that Friday was the best day, as both the kids and
I anticipated the weekend too much to do anything
very formal anyway. To keep Games Day lively, I put
out a new game on the "Game of the Week" shelf each
Monday. This gives my students something to look forward to during the week. On Friday, the new game is
added to the others in the games cabinet, and the next
Monday I put another new game on the shelf.

In addition to Fridays, each of my classes has three
Games Certificate Days. At the beginning of the year
I give the president of each class certificates that may

be redeemed for a games day on a day that would normally be used for reading. The reason for this is two-fold. First, it gives the students a chance to participate in "democracy," not the democracy of who-gets-to-hand-out-the-textbooks-nobody-wants-to-read, but the real-life arguing and dealing that enters into any group consensus. Second, I give the certificates because there are inevitably going to be a few days during the year when a class just won't feel like doing any work. Maybe because gang tensions are high, or because they took a big test the period before they came to me, or for some reason that I'm not even aware of. If a class feels strongly enough about not working to use one of their precious three certificates, I probably couldn't have conducted a regular class anyway.

A final word. In the previous chapter I noted that to maintain classroom order the urban teacher had to create "something to lose." Games are a part of this "something," but that doesn't mean that they should be used as a disciplinary lever or as a reward for suffering through less exciting material. On their own, games will contribute substantially to a "give some—get some" atmosphere in a classroom. I give my students a lot, but I expect an equal amount in return. I expect them to learn to read.

3

THE BASIC: READING

The other afternoon, while browsing through children's books in a Philadelphia store, I overheard a salesman asking a twelve-year-old customer what he wanted. The youngster said that he'd "like a good, exciting mystery book." "How about Alfred Hitchcock's *Stories for Late at Night?*" he was asked. "Naw," said the boy, "I've already read that one. What else've you got?"

The most mundane, ordinary type of conversation— except to me. I'm surprised that any child can read Hitchcock. Certainly the fourteen-year-olds that I teach cannot. Of the 150 eighth-graders I have this year, which includes the 60 students in the "academically advanced" sections, *only three* can read at an eighth-grade level. Over 50 of the other 147 cannot read a book written at above a third-grade level (as measured by the Stanford Reading Achievement Test).

The increasingly publicized gap between national "norms" and the reading test results of ghetto children is much more than just numbers. A student with a fourth-grade reading ability can comfortably handle this:

> "Let's go up to the hillside today,
> To play, to play,
> To play,
> Up to the hill where the daisies grow,
> Like snow, like snow,
> Like snow."

> (From *Round the Corner*, a basal text in The Bank Street Readers, The Macmillan Company, 1966. In my opinion the best basal reading series now available.)

An eighth-grade student reading at his proper level, though, has no difficulty at all with this passage from *The Autobiography of Malcolm X*:

> "All through the war the Harlem racial picture never was too bright. Tension built to a pretty high pitch. Old-timers told me that Harlem had never been the same since the 1935 riot."

If the world had gone completely McLuhan by now, this gap would make no difference, and we'd all be "watching" Malcolm X instead of reading his book. But, because nonlinear communication has yet to replace the printed word, the ability to read must—repeat twice and underline—must transcend every other learnable skill. Until ghetto students learn to read, the teaching of any other academic discipline in a slum school is an unsupportable delusion.

A math teacher cannot expect his students to figure out whether Train A will pass Train B three hours out of the station at X miles per hour if his students can't read the problem. A science teacher cannot expect her students to extract oxygen from the atmosphere if they can't read the procedures for setting up the experiment. It's true that if the science teacher could find a different way to do the experiment, her students might be able to work a little chemistry. But it's equally true that that knowledge wouldn't help them figure out at what point Train A will pass Train B. Reading, though, allows a student to do both, and more. Essentially, it gives him the opportunity to learn what he wants to learn. Without it, despite his desire, there is little that he can learn.

This emphasis on reading is not a novel concept, yet the fact remains that a twelve-year-old suburban child can read books that are too difficult for most urban high school graduates. Why is this the case, when the process of learning to read, be it in Scarsdale or in Watts, is identical for both children?

Reading, to begin with, is the ability to decode and translate symbols into sounds. It is nothing more than that. It is *not* comprehension, interpretation, extrapolation, or any of the myriad of other skills that teachers tend to confuse it with. Being able to draw conclusions and inferences from presented material, for example, are skills in themselves. They apply to any situation or subject, and shouldn't be considered the domain of reading teachers. (For a penetrating analysis of this argument, see James Moffett's *A Student-centered Language Arts Curriculum*, Houghton Mifflin Company, 1968.)

In other words, if you can say, "Lirute en quartine regmire wiselbang," you can read.

Having decoded, you are ready for the second step, which is understanding. "Lirute . . . wiselbang," in our particular code, means "The batter hit the pitched ball." If you even remotely know the game of baseball, you've had sufficient life experience to comprehend what you've read. But if you've never seen, heard of, nor in any other way participated in the sport, to you it remains "wiselbang." (This life experience is one of the antecedents to learning those thinking skills so often confused with reading ability.)

Decoding and having life experience mean little, of course, if you don't care to read about baseball. The third and last step is desire.

Suburban children learn to decode in the early grades, either through the sight method—learning whole words and recognizing them through constant repetition in pictured contexts—or through the phonic method—pronouncing the sounds of different combinations of letters—or through some mixture of the two. (The effectiveness of each technique is definitively reviewed in Jeanne Chall's *Learning to Read: The Great Debate*, McGraw-Hill Book Company, Inc., 1967.)

Suburban students have life experience. They've been to camp, on a subway, to a bowling alley, they know what a lawn looks like, know how to hold a tennis racquet. In addition, suburban parents verbally pass on their own experiences to their children.

Finally, middle-class youngsters have a generally healthy attitude toward books. They were read to when

young and grow up realizing that books can be one of
life's pleasures.

As a group, suburban students can read. (Some, of
course, can't, but for reasons completely unrelated to
those which affect the slum student. Many suburban
children react to incessant pressure to read at an increasingly younger age by not reading at all. But this
is an emotional, not a reading, problem.)

In contrast there are the children I teach. At least 25
percent of them cannot decode. Their elementary
teachers didn't properly instruct them. Having thirty-
five children say phonetic sounds in unison or using
independent small-group instruction would only have encouraged discipline problems. Instead, these teachers
had their pupils silently color in pictures of animals, fill-
ing in the blank between the *B* and the *T*, a poor substitute.

Seventy-five percent of my students can decode, but
most of them have meager life experience. Read all the
phrases that hide the blemish but don't make the neces-
say dietetic changes, "underprivileged," "deprived," etc.
Too many of my children have never been outside the
square-mile area between home and school. Last year, for
instance, I took a group of boys to watch the Philadelphia '76ers play basketball against the Los Angeles
Lakers. The Spectrum sports arena was about an hour
away from our meeting place. After what seemed an in-
terminable ride on the subway, the boys and I transferred to a bus. As we alighted, eleven stops later, one of
the young men looked around and in all seriousness
asked me, "Are we in Canada yet?"

Some of my students, perhaps as many a fifty out of 150, can read. They just don't want to. Where have they ever seen a good book? Not at home, where there are few, if any, and not in school, where most textbooks are about as exciting as seeing Andy Warhol's film *Sleep* for the third time.

The urban teacher, then, is faced with this three-part combination: students who cannot decode, those who can but who lack the experience necessary to understand what they've read, and those who are convinced that a good book doesn't exist. What should he do?

During my first year I fell into the pit called Compensatory Reading. Compensatory Reading means you get federal funds to buy dull fourth-grade textbooks for illiterate eighth-graders, instead of dull eighth-grade texts. Being a social studies teacher, I substituted the advanced history book with an elementary one. The obvious occurred. I lost every student who couldn't read fourth-grade words, lost the few students who found the book too easy, and lost everyone else because it was, to understate the quality of the text, a little dry.

During the summer between my first and second years I made an important decision—that to try to teach social studies to children who couldn't read was a waste of my effort and their time. I decided, with the help of a sympathetic principal, to teach reading instead. I began by trying to analyze the reading problem beyond the "compensatory" stage. It appeared to me (and still does) that people read for one of a combination of two reasons, either for enjoyment and entertainment, be it Harold Robbins or Søren Kierkegaard, or to obtain information needed to solve a problem. But I've yet to meet the business executive who goes to his office and for no reason at all reads pages 12 to 23 and answers the questions at the bottom of page 24.

Children, too, will read for pleasure and/or information, but both approaches require certain prerequisites.

First, the reading matter must be at the child's level. This is so obvious that mentioning it once is redundant, but most teachers find something embarrassing about issuing second-grade books to fourteen-year-olds. A while ago, I had the opportunity of addressing reading teachers on this question. Instead of opening the discussion with the hackneyed "Let's talk about reading," I gave each the following classroom assignment from Jean-Paul Sartre's *Being and Nothingness:*

DIRECTIONS: Read the following passage, and answer the questions at the bottom of the page.

"The future is the determining being which the For-Itself has to be beyond being. There is a future because the For-Itself has to be it's being instead of simply being it. This being which the For-Itself has to be cannot be in the mode of the co-present in-itselfs; for in that case it would be without being made to be; we could not then imagine it as a completely designed state to which presence alone would be lacking, as Kant says that existence adds nothing more to the object of the concept."

1. How does Kant feel about objects?
2. Why do you think so?

3. What is the "For-Itself"? (*In your own words!*)

Second, slum children must be rewarded for their reading efforts in the immediate present. Middle-class students know that a Mustang, split-level home, and social acceptance await the end of the road, and this provides them enough motivation to sit through much of what passes for education in the suburbs. Ghetto students have no such incentives, so some substitute must be used.

Third, the children must be free to talk—absolutely an essential for those students who must check their decoding against reality.

Finally, for black students, the content of the books must be closely scrutinized. Many old books have racially condescending material—"There were even three Negroes there"—and much of the tremendous volume of hurriedly prepared new material presents only Stepin Fetchit stereotypes.

Keeping these prerequisites in mind, I elected to try the Reading for Pleasure/Reward method during my second year.

The initial step was to convince all the children that books were enjoyable and a satisfying experience. If they weren't, then students who couldn't decode wouldn't try to, and students who could read but didn't want to, wouldn't.

To accomplish this, I literally stuffed the room full of exciting, new books, from the simplest squeeze-me-and-I-make-a-noise cloth ones to *Manchild in the Promised Land*. (See Chapter 9 for financing book purchases.) Colorful, exciting volumes on gangs, race, sports, sex,

fairy tales, the gamut of the Dewey Decimal System. I
made sure that I (*a*) excluded anything that might be
construed as a text and (*b*) included all those controver-
sial titles which the vice-principal warned me to keep out.
Then I told the kids to "walk around the room. Pick out
any book that looks exciting to you. Read it, either by
yourself or with a friend. If it turns out that it's a crummy
book, return it and get another. There will be no tests,
reports, or questions of any kind about anything you
have read."

The children reacted cautiously. Was I sure that there
would be no tests? Positively no book reports? You didn't
have to know the author, publisher, and copyright date?
Even reassured, the kids were hesitant. Why should my
room be different from their other teachers'? All the
students proceeded to select the hardest books they could
find. They would prove to me that they didn't need
"baby books like Dr. Seuss." So they sat through the first
two or three days professionally thumbing through in-
comprehensible pages. Nor did I exhort any child who
could only read *Little Red Riding Hood* to put his copy
of *Invisible Man* back on the shelf. The student knew
he couldn't read, and he didn't need the ego deflation of
being reminded of it.

As the weeks wore on, my students became more trust-
ing. There hadn't been a test, had there? By the end of
the month, the squeeze-me books were squeaking.

During this initial period, a teacher from down the
hall kept popping into my room. On her third "pop" she
asked me to justify letting the kids read such childish
books as *Bambi*. How could they learn anything? I bet
her the quarter I'd recently won on the geography puz-

zle experiment that any student she chose couldn't read three straight lines of *Bambi* without a significant error. She picked a student who fumbled on "regarded," and I was up to fifty cents.

At the beginning of the second month, I divided each of my classes into five or six homogeneous groups, from nondecoders to Malcolm Xers. Knowing that I couldn't simultaneously teach six groups, I appointed students to act as teachers (initially those children who had challenged my authority at the start of the year, a constructive outlet for their desire to lead). After the first month, these teachers were rotated so that everyone got a chance. Each student-teacher was to lead his group in the study of the basal reader which I had assigned for their particular level.

Grouping is a device that more teachers would use if they were sure that it wouldn't increase their discipline troubles, for nobody can have both eyes in four different corners of the room at the same time. Circumventing this problem isn't too difficult, but it requires that the teacher relinquish direct control of his class, something that most teachers are too insecure to try. Many teachers ask students to lead groups, but the breakdown occurs when classmates mistreat the student-teacher. The reason they can do this is that the teacher gives his student-teacher responsibility, but no authority with which to fulfill it. In my class, since he was completely responsible for the group's progress, the student-teacher had total authority over the group. Whether they read their text aloud or silently, front to back or back to front, or in rotation, was up to the student-teacher. He decided who could be excused to go to the bathroom, who had permission to get a drink of water, and who would be suspended from school for misconduct.

The student-teacher's power, however, was not arbitrary. It had a natural base, for the teacher of a third grade level group, for example, would himself be a fourth-grade reader. Self-protection ensured that the student-teacher would not abuse his power. He still had to walk out of the building with any student he suspended.

A typical "reading day" went like this. The kids "drove" their chairs, in bumper-car fashion, to their respective corners. At the same time the student-teacher got the texts, and the Word-Looker-Upper of each group (appointed by the student-teacher) got the group's notebook. As the group read, the Looker-Upper wrote down the definitions of words they didn't understand. At the end of half an hour, the books were returned and the chairs were bruised back into their original positions.

The classroom atmosphere on a reading day was one of laxity and freedom. Just the simple action of moving chairs around provided a physical release, and since the kids were responsible to a student-teacher instead of a teacher-teacher, there was little mental pressure.

During this reading period I would spend half my time with the nondecoders and the other half testing groups who had completed their text. These tests were oral, and were composed of recall questions on the stories and word definitions from the group's notebook. If a group passed, they progressed to the next higher reader in the series, and they moved up on the Reading Progress Board.

The Reading Progress Board was one of the external motivational devices that I used to encourage the children's reading. One wall of the room was covered with dark Portuguese cork. Each student had his name affixed along the bottom, with a colored map-flag pinned over it. As his group finished a book and passed the test, his flag advanced two of the twelve total spaces on the board. If he reached the top by the end of the school year, he was appropriately rewarded—a giant Sugar Daddy candy sucker.

Another incentive that was very effective was the "Group of the Week." The best group each week (a subjective decision, as are most decisions) had its picture taken in full color. The photograph was posted on the wall, and each child got a Hershey bar. A well-read classroom marches on its stomach!

In addition to the board and photos, I recorded the children's reading. Hearing their own voices was a real thrill. A tape recorder, by the way, is much more than a motivational technique, as I discovered in the case of Henry Harris. Henry had the widest lisp outside of the Castillian coast of Spain. The school's visiting speech therapist told me that he refused to come to her for assistance. Instead of forcing him to go, and causing him to become even more defensive, I recorded his group every couple of weeks. By the eighth or ninth session, Henry admitted to his lisp, and asked for help. Today, two years later, he still adds a slight 's' to every word, but his speech is far more coherent.

The readers were good, the motivations excellent, and the entire approach worked out well. Statistically, the 150 children gained about 60 percent more in reading ability than what their "naturally expected gain" would have been. This increase, though impressive, didn't seem high enough to me. Another summer analysis gave me new answers as to why.

Although I had realized that all thirty students wouldn't want to read the same book, I hadn't carried this line of thought to its logical conclusion. There probably weren't more than two or three students in each group who liked their assigned text. (Student reaction to the readers is in the Appendix.)

Also, I had dishonestly tricked my kids into using texts by urging them to read nontexts before the program started. (How many teachers use a half grain of motivation to open a student's mouth, then force-feed him a quart of castor oil?)

Then (a holdover from my own school days) I had made the dictionary definition of words mandatory. Until reading John Holt's *The Under-achieving School* (Pitman Publishing Corporation, 1969), I wasn't aware that I, like most adults, don't look up words I don't know. I figure them out from context. If I had to stop every time I found a new word, I'm sure I'd never get through a book.

Worse than anything else, though, I had tested the kids on their knowledge of the definitions, and I had tested them on the material itself. Had the reading been interesting enough, I wouldn't have found this kind of "checking" necessary. In effect, I had forced their recall of information that they didn't want, and would undoubtedly forget as soon as the test was over. Impossibility Number One is trying to teach something to somebody who doesn't want to learn it!

During my third year (and thereafter), I set up a completely individualized program. I obtained two copies of each of close to three hundred different books and divided them into six levels of difficulty. All the children who read at any one level form that level group. The difference in approach is that a student reads only what he wants to read, not what I have imposed on him. On a reading day, he goes over to his level's bookcase, selects any book and then, either alone or with someone else in his group, reads it.

During a typical class period, students are reading widely divergent material. In Group One (a reading level between 0.1 and about 1.5), he might be looking at *Green Eggs and Ham* or *One Fish Two Fish Red Fish Blue Fish*, both Dr. Seuss books. In Group Two (1.3 to 3.0), any part of the Babar series, or perhaps *The Travels of Dr. Dolittle*. In Group Three (2.6 to 4.5), *My Brother Stevie*, the story of a young girl who has to take care of her baby brother while her mother is away, a typical situation for many of my students, or *Martin Luther King: Courageous Warrior*. In Group Four (4.0 to 5.5), a student may be reading *Lilies of the Field* or *The Soul Brothers and Sister Lou*, one of the most popular books in the room, about a young girl whose friends drop out of school, start a gang, get in trouble with the police, but who, *deus ex machina*, end up forming a successful singing group. In Group Five (5.5 and up), *Anything for a Friend*, the story of a young middle-class white girl's efforts to integrate the senior prom by having one of her suitors take the small New England town's only black girl, or *More Stories from The Twilight Zone*. In Group Six (7.0 and up), a student could choose to read *Malcolm X Speaks*, or, if she's a girl, she might enjoy *Escape from Nowhere*, the tale of a teen-ager on drugs. Whatever the book, there isn't one that is less motivating and relevant

than *Our American Story*, or some similarly titled eighth-
grade history book. (A complete list of books on each
level, including notes as to which are the most popular, which are racially balanced, and so forth, is in Chapter 11.)

If on a given day a student chooses not to read, he
doesn't. Instead of getting his book, he goes over to my
desk, which since my second year has been tucked in a
far corner of the room, and he sits and does nothing. The
students have nicknamed this part of the room the "Do
Nothing Corner." The corner is not a retreat for students
who never want to read (which rarely happens if they're
given an almost unlimited choice of books), but for any
child who on a particular day "just don't feel like it."

It's true that I could "force" the child to read—rather
to look like he was reading. I can make him sit still, and I
can make him put the open book before his open eyes,
but I cannot make him move his eyes over the page.
Further, this kind of "force" will only antagonize the
child. If I continue to compel what won't come naturally,
I am as much as sending out an engraved invitation for
a discipline problem. Everybody has their off days. Most
adults call in sick. Children should have the same opportunity.

When a student finishes a book, he goes over to the
room's file box and writes on his card the name of the
book and the date he completed it. Then he goes back to
his level's bookcase and picks out another book, which
he starts to read. To progress from one level group to
another, a student must read a specified number of books,
20 out of 40 in the most elementary level, 5 out of 45 in the
highest. If a student can't find any book that appeals to
him, I take him to the public library after school.

I continue to use student-teachers, but their role is now limited to assisting with word definitions. If a student has trouble with a word, he asks his student-teacher for help. If neither of them knows the word, they ask me. And if the three of us can't define it, we go to the dictionary. Otherwise, I spend my time with the group of nondecoders.

I still use the Reading Progress Board and the payoff of a giant Sugar Daddy at the end of the year for students who reach the top, but I've dropped taking and posting pictures. The content of the books more than compensates for them.

Since my students read only books that they like, testing is superfluous. Statistically, the results of this program are astounding.

In September, 1969, I gave my students a standardized reading test. The average score was 4.5, which means that my eighth-graders were collectively reading at a level equivalent to that of a student halfway through the fourth grade. On the basis of past performance I could reasonably expect that by the end of the year my students would be reading at exactly a fifth-grade level. In other words, over their past seven years in school, this group had a tendency to gain about six months for every ten months of school. If nothing changed, then, they would improve from 4.5 to 5.0 at the end of their first nine months with me. Instead, post-testing in May, 1970, showed that the average had increased to 5.7. (A complete breakdown of test results appears in the Appendix.) This means that the 127 tested students had improved 130 percent more than could have been reasonably expected. This was more than twice as much progress as the year-earlier "grouped reading" had produced. On top of that, this gain beat the national average for growth in reading ability by 30 percent, which includes all schools, suburban as well as ghetto. Quite a remarkable performance!

The Pleasure/Reward approach to reading, as excellent as I have found it, is not perfect. Nondecoders can be helped by a teacher who now has free time, and students who have the ability to read now have the desire. But children who have insufficient life experience—even if they read books that reflect that experience—don't significantly enlarge it. Their background can be broadened, though, by the second approach to reading, Problem-Solving.

Solving a problem in real life requires reading. As John R. Seeley, in his article "Remaking the Urban Scene" (*Daedalus,* Vol. 97, No. 4, Fall, 1968), points out: "Whatever corresponds to skills will appear as natural emergents from activities and experiences creditable and valuable in their own general terms. . . . Put another way, the way of life will engender the skills that enhance it."

The problems that a teacher and his class attempt to solve must be significant ones to the students. If they become the same old "I wonder how a bill passes Congress," the students will react with their same old disinterest and misbehavior. But if the group decides to produce and give out to the community a handbook of phone numbers to call to complain about poor housing, rats, and discrimination in public places, there will be real interest. This project, by the way, was successfully undertaken in Harlem.

Another real-life problem is the favorite of a friend of mine, Gary Richardson. He signs his junior high school class out of school "on a trip," and loads his kids into a chartered bus. Each child is given two transportation tokens, ten cents, and a map of the city. Then they are blindfolded. The bus takes them to the outskirts of the city, dropping one in a dead end here, another in the middle of a park there, and so on until all of them have been left off. The first student to reach City Hall (in the center of Philadelphia) wins. A great game, and the signs and maps are real reading. Furthermore, going to the outskirts of the city is a longer trip from home than many of his students have ever taken. Parenthetically, his answer to the inevitable question is "No." He's "brought them all back alive" and happy.

Both approaches to reading can be combined. Classroom Reading for Pleasure can be enlivened with many of the special projects and activities described in the next chapter. And Problem-Solving can take place in the classroom—reading through the city charter, for example, to find out which office is responsible for the buses running late or why ghetto streets are always so filthy.

Having students write stories on consequential subjects, not their four hundredth "What I Want to Be When I Grow Up," but "What's Wrong (or Right) with the Housing Project I Live In" integrates both methods. Last year, for example, I asked every child to write a short, short story. Some correcting, a little practice duplicating, and presto, thirty copies of a book, which the class read. Most of the stories were autobiographical. Some were humorous:

"I got up and went to look for my shoes. I looked all over the house, but I couldn't find them. Then, my brother came and told me that the dog had them. So I went to find the dog. I found the dog under the chair, trying to take the string out of them. I was still asleep, so I picked up that dog and asked him if he was looking for a fight. I think he said no, but just in case I threw him around the room. Then I went back."

Other stories were not so cute:

"This damned school makes me tired of looking at it. One day I will do all those things my mother always told me not to do. I will not go to school. I know that I will not go back. If you ever get left down [retained a year], those damned teachers make a big deal out of it."

(For examples of eloquent writing by slum children, I highly commend editor Stephen Joseph's *The Me Nobody Knows: Children's Voices from the Ghetto*, Avon Books, 1969.)

Reading for Pleasure or Reading to Solve a Problem— it doesn't matter which. What does matter is that these children *can* be taught to read. And I invite those skeptical teachers who think "it can't be done" to talk with Willie Smith.

Willie, a large, strapping young man who preferred cutting classes to sitting in them, was a student of mine for two years. At the start of the seventh grade he had a reading level of 3.2. He wasn't interested in reading at all until well into the third month of school, when he happened to see a classmate reading *Paul Bunyan*. *Paul Bunyan* started Willie on a two-year reading jag that included countless tall tales and biographies. By the end of the seventh grade, his reading level had shot up to 5.7. Testing at the end of the eighth grade showed that his reading level had further increased to 7.3, a total gain of over four years in under twenty months.

4

"SPIT IT OUT, STANLEY!"

It's the Wednesday before the Thursday-Friday Thanksgiving break. Around the school, teachers are giving one of the tests they invariably allocate for the day right before a holiday. Their students are responding in their usual inimitable fashion: Most, wishing that the bell would ring, sit staring at the clock. Others sleep, their heads propped up by the arm that crinkles the test sheet. Some, more honest, make a missile of the page and fly it out the window.

In my room also, students sit with a "test" in front of them. But they study it intently, very much concerned that they get the right answer. It's a real problem. How many inches will Reginald the Paper Turkey "fly" before he's shot down? They write down a number and turn it in. Then Reginald, hanging at the top of a diagonally slanted wire that stretches across the room, is released. He flies down the wire until I shoot the cap pistol, which is the signal for my student assistant to stop him. The student whose guess comes closest to the distance Reginald actually flew wins a twenty-five-cent chocolate turkey.

In October, it's Halloween. Children, looking forward to the aching stomach that follows the collection of pounds of candy, are paying absolutely no attention to their teachers. But in my room they're squinting through the darkness to see how many times Penelope Pumpkin will wink before she shuts her eyes to go to sleep. Penelope, a regularly carved pumpkin, has a blue light bulb in her cranium. The student who comes closest to guessing the number of times she'll flash wins a half dozen pumpkin cupcakes. (Ideas for other holiday games are in Chapter 11.)

If a teacher feels it necessary to give tests at all, he should at least give his students the benefit of optimum timing. The day before Christmas is no time to try to test or summarize important material.

Timing and variations in a repetitive curriculum are arts that a masterful teacher can use to improve the flavor of his children's entire school year. He shouldn't, for instance, present his most exciting material in September, when the novelty of a new term is enough by itself to sustain momentum, but should hold it instead for the winter, when the weather may be poor, when there isn't another vacation to anticipate, and when June seems as remote as the millennium.

In my class I try to make those dead months less ignorable by injecting special projects. Last January, for example, I bought three dozen instamatic-type cameras (44 cents each), and asked the kids to script and photograph a short story. The scripts were highly imaginative. Mr. Jones pretends to die in a car crash and gets sent to the morgue. His wife collects the insurance money, but Mr. Jones "comes back from the dead" to haunt her. Mrs. Jones dies of fright, and Mr. Jones runs away with his mistress, who turns out to be Mrs. Jones's sister. End of story. The quality of the children's photos didn't match their writing, as very few had had previous experience with a camera. So I invited a professional photographer to come to school to explain how to shoot and develop pictures.

In February my classes started painting "The Endless Mural." I bought a long roll of coarse brown wrapping paper, five gallons of paint, and thirty small brushes. I suggested that each class work together on one long mural, but met objection from many of the kids who wanted to work alone. We compromised—the children could work either singly or in groups. Some groups were as large as eight, and a couple of the murals stretched out thirty feet. The only "assignment" involved in the project was that each child write one sentence at the bottom of his painting explaining what it was.

In March the students wrote plays and then videotaped them on the school's federally donated television equipment.

During April the children worked on the "What I Love or Hate" project. Task: "Describe to me, in pictures, something you love or hate. If possible, also in pictures, tell me why." The children brought in stacks of old magazines, and I provided construction paper, tape, scissors, and glue.

On weeks when there is no special project, I try to have one day of something out of the ordinary. This year Tuesday through Thursday are reserved for reading (neutral days), the children get Friday for games (their day), and I get Monday. I try to vary my Monday activities enough so that students who like neither reading nor games can at least have something to enjoy. Often I play games such as Ten Clues, which directly teach vocabulary and indirectly teach imaginative thinking.

DIRECTIONS: As soon as you can identify what it is, write down your answer on a sheet of scrap paper and turn it in. Only one guess per person. First five people with the correct answer win.

1. It can sit, but not move around.
2. You can smell it, but not hear it.
3. Many people would say that it's the same as a nasty remark you'd make about an elderly woman.
4. It has a string, but you can't fly it.
5. It starts dry, but ends up wet.
6. Most people won't take it unless its color is changed.
7. In order for it to work properly, it must have a container.
8. It only works if water is added to it.

9. It can be used more than once, but only a
   miser would use it three times.
10. It sounds like a letter in the alphabet, but you
   can't "c" it.

(The answer is on the last page of this chapter.)

On other Mondays, I bring in classroom visitors, but
not the stereotypical maiden aunt who prattles on for
an hour about her impressions of the Acropolis, and
certainly not the police community relations team who
tells us how friendly they are, when from the window
of my room we can see the same police brutally frisking
the older brother of one of the kids. Some of last year's
guests included a hairdresser who demonstrated styling
technique on one girl in each class, a fashion model who
demonstrated the correct way to wear clothing, walk,
and pose, an "Old Head" gang member who described
the inside of the city jail, and so forth. Aside from being
entertaining, my students could identify with black people who had "made it" (in both senses).

The activity that my students enjoy most, however, is
role-playing and psychodrama. Psychodrama, the creation
of Dr. J. L. Moreno of Beacon, New York, is a combination of sociological role-playing and psychological group
therapy. It permits the students to get out their feelings
toward me, school, one another, racism, gangs, sex, or
any other subject. In classroom form, it calls for setting
up a wide circle of chairs, with two chairs in the middle,
on the "stage." All the students in the class sit in the
circle, and any student who wants to talk, or in any
other way act out his feelings, is free to come and sit

in (stand, walk around) one of the middle chairs. He can ask someone else to sit in the other chair, or the other chair can remain empty. On occasion, more chairs are moved into the center. The lighting and staging effects are controlled by a director (usually myself). Audience participation is encouraged at all times, and the only restriction governing psychodrama in my room is that there be no physical violence.

The most exciting psychodrama I personally participated in occurred with Stanley Frazier during my first year. Of all the control problems I had that year, Stanley was the biggest. Incessantly talking, leaving the room as though it were a movie house and he wanted more popcorn, chewing gum until I was convinced he'd need false teeth. (A year later, recalling that there were some college classes I couldn't get through without a cigarette, I changed my mind about the value of chewing gum.)

On a Monday in the middle of the year, lights dimmed, Stanley moved to one of the center chairs. He asked me to share the stage with him. Then he loudly announced that he was going to be the teacher, and that I should act as Stanley. I agreed, walked over to one of his classmates, asked for a stick of gum, and returned to my chair. Then, as elaborately as possible, I unwrapped the gum, stuck it in my mouth, and threw the wrapper on the floor. Stanley, acting very much the teacher, stood up, approached my chair, and said, "Spit it out." I continued chewing. "Spit it out!" he said, pointing a finger at me. I did nothing. He wheeled, walked over to the corner of the room, brought back the wastepaper basket, and with all the authority he could muster, firmly spoke: "Stanley, I want you to pick up your wrapper, put your

gum in it, and throw them in this basket!" Still, I did
nothing. Stanley looked at his classmates in the circle,
then looked back at me. There wasn't a sound in the
room. Quietly he put the wastepaper basket back in the
corner and returned to his seat in the circle.

An impressive lesson. Without physical force, you can't
make a ghetto student do something which he vehemently refuses to do. Superficially, I learned that teacher-
baiting can be fun, and Stanley found out what it was
like to be faced with a Stanley in his class. Not surprisingly, his misbehavior through the end of the year was
minimal.

Another psychodrama concerned gang wars. Two members of one gang sat across from and confronted two
members of another gang. Since physical violence was
against the rules, the language was pretty strong. Though
most of the interplay centered around who had the
stronger gang—regardless of who was playing which
role—it came out in one long exchange that one of the
reasons most kids join gangs is fear: fear that they will
be socially ostracized if they don't, and fear for their
physical safety if they remain independent.

While a few psychodramas in one classroom didn't
stop gang wars in Philadelphia, the lesson that joining
gangs is a product of weakness and not of strength is
something I could never formally teach.

Role-playing, while not as psychologically involving
as psychodrama, is just as stimulating. One Monday
during my second year the room was turned into Munici-
pal Court #407. The defendant, Alan Jenkins, was an ex-
troverted, good-looking boy. He was charged with cutting school for two days (which was true). Alan wasn't

particularly embarrassed at being singled out for this offense, as most kids cut at one time or another during the year. If anything, he was a little proud of it.

After Alan was sworn in, Robert Coleman, the prosecuting attorney, started the interrogation:

> "How come you cut? You know you can't get a job without an education."
>
> Alan didn't say anything.
>
> Robert (more impatient): "You ain't gonna get nowhere if you cut. Man, if you skip school—"
>
> Defense attorney Keith Morton interjected: "You don't learn nothin' at school. You can learn more outa here. How do you know you can't get a job, huh?"
>
> Robert: "Listen, I know."
>
> Keith: "How do you know?"
>
> Robert: "Listen, man, I know!"

After two minutes of this the judge, another student, quieted everybody down. Then he leaned over his desk and queried Alan directly:

> Judge: "Whad'ja learn outa school?"
>
> Alan: "Nothin' much."
>
> Judge: "Whad'ja do?"
>
> Alan: "Walked around and played sports."
>
> Judge: "Don'cha know it's against the law to cut school?"

Finally, the case went to the jury, which was composed of the rest of the class. They returned a verdict of "guilty as charged," but recommended probation. They further ordered that if Alan cut again, he "be made to stay after school one hour a day for a week," in effect making up the time he was out.

This warning proved effective. Either Alan didn't cut again or he had the sense to have the same person forge all his absence excuses.

(Answer to Ten Clues: A TEA BAG.)

5

WHEN DOES THE SCHOOL DAY END?

As the sound of the final bell of the day approaches, most classrooms take on the appearance of a track field. At about ten minutes to three, the teacher starts inconspicuously wandering toward his coat locker, and the students begin surreptitiously tucking their papers and texts into their looseleaf notebooks. By five minutes to three, the teacher has casually draped his coat over his arm, and students, finished arranging their books, lean forward in their seats. As the gong sounds, the teacher jumps into his coat, the students jump out of their chairs, and the race begins. Elementary school teachers have an unfair advantage: their stride is longer than their students', and they easily win. In secondary schools it's closer.

In a silent but obvious way, both sets of competitors have announced their feeling toward school. It's a place to get out of, the quicker, the better. Which is, of course, quite contrary to the very vocal announcement that teachers make during the day, that school is a tremendously beneficial place to spend time. (Never mind the irony of detentions. If school were truly that great, would one of the most effective penalties for misbehavior be keeping a student in a place he liked?)

By 3:10 the building is empty. The sound of constant movement has been replaced by the aimless swish of the janitor's broom. There's nothing more to write on the board, no more forms to be completed, and any teacher still in the school will probably be sitting down and trying to unwind. While he relaxes, one or two of his students may wander in. And at that moment the teacher and his pupil become people, not just ships that pass in the afternoon. Mr. Ryan, for example, may find out that Harold fell asleep in class because his mother's sick and in the hospital, and he's burdened with the responsibility of a house full of younger brothers and sisters. Harold, in the same way, may discover that Mr. Ryan is a real, live, perhaps chronologically over the hill, but nonetheless *human*, being; that he wasn't born with a tie jutting from his neck; that, like others, he smokes the cigarettes that he cautions his students against; and that maybe he does care about his kids.

But this kind of personal interaction—which is *Education* with the capital *E*—cannot occur within the confines of the present nine-to-three system, for a teacher with a normal load—30 to 35 students every 43 minutes— can spend only 73 seconds with each child each day. That's if he's worked out an individualized program. If, as is usually the case, he's formally leading (or lecturing) his class, he's cut his "time per pupil" to three or four seconds. This situation inevitably leads to the question: How significant can any teacher's influence on his students be in 3, or even 73, seconds a day?

But a teacher who remains after school for half an hour, or who spends a weekend afternoon with his students, can have a profound influence on them. One Saturday from noon to six triples the total amount of time a teacher spends with a student during the entire school year.

Such thinking led me to invite all my students to join me for a day in the park. The boys and I would play football, and the girls would make picnic lunches. There was wild enthusiasm for the idea. We talked about it all week, which girl would make which lunch, and which boy would be on which team. On Friday, I asked how many of them would be meeting me in front of the school the following morning. About a hundred. This seemed a little high, and as I turned the corner to school on Saturday, I expected to see only thirty or forty.

Johnny McWilliams sat alone on the front steps. I looked around the block again, maybe the kids had confused the corner? Then I asked Johnny what time I had said we'd meet. At 11:00, he confirmed. It was 11:10. I told him that I must have mixed up the times, and that the rest of the kids would show up at noon. So we sat and waited. Nobody came. With an awfully empty feeling in my stomach, I asked Johnny why *he* had come? Being with an adult, he said, was the only way he could be let out of his foster home on a Saturday.

Johnny and I went to the park, threw the football around, and ate lunch. It was a thoroughly miserable day.

A couple of weeks later, after the hurt had subsided, I tried to examine what had gone wrong. In doing so, I remembered the advice my mother once offered about trying to date a girl who was indifferent toward me. "Call her up and tell her you have two tickets to a great play, and does she want to go with you? That way, if she doesn't like you, she might go along to see the play. Then you have an opening." Similarly, my students didn't need me to take them to the park, they could go by themselves. Anyway, why should they spend their Saturday with a teacher they saw all week in school?

So I wrote the Philadelphia Flyers ice hockey team for ten complimentary tickets to a Friday night game. They sent them, and seven boys came.

A local movie house agreed to discount tickets to *Around the World in Eighty Days,* and fifteen children came.

Next, I asked half a dozen students if they wanted to come to a downtown store with me to pick out games and toys for the classroom. (Why order sight-unseen material from a catalog when what the children select themselves will be more effective?) The six children turned into twenty-five, and what a contrast it was with that bleak afternoon with Johnny McWilliams! Two dozen children, some of whose parents don't have enough money for toys, were encouraged to run through Woolworth's, picking out anything at all they wanted. It was like winning one of those "$100.00 a month for life" contests.

These and other outings showed my kids what I was like in "my world" (and in addition slightly increased the life experience they need for reading). But I also wanted to find out what they were like in "their world." One Friday afternoon, I plotted out my student's addresses on a city map. The next afternoon I "just happened" to be walking through their neighborhood with a bat and ball. The result was a two-hour baseball game and an invitation to return the next week to play again.

The more I learned about the children, the more I understood that as much as they disliked school, they had nowhere else to go. They are shuttled from the business district by store managers who pall at the sight of black teen-agers who are "only looking." There are many locally funded July and August projects that the children enjoy, but as soon as the threat of the "long, hot summer" disappears, the money hibernates until spring.

So, at the last school bell, the students carefully wend their way home. There, they spend the rest of the afternoon playing in the "safe" (from gangs) streets, or watching television. But after a while, even TV can get dull.

For those reasons I decided to set up a 45-minute after-school program in my room. I bought leather-craft wallet kits, imitation beads and stones for making bracelets and necklaces, wood-carving sets, and other arts and crafts materials.

I also created a very large and somewhat special lending library, with books like *I Spy* and *Bonanza*. (Better a well-read *Hawaii Five-O* than an unopened *Silas Marner*.) What is special is that the books don't have to be checked out, a student just takes what he wants. I trust him to return it. The library also lends out cameras on the honor system.

From the outset the afterschool program was well received. By 3:05 there is always a line of thirty-five or forty students waiting to get into the room. Once in, they work on their arts and crafts projects until the last minute, keeping what they finish. But the library is the star attraction. The turnover rate of the 2,000 books is close to 30 percent a month. The theft rate runs about 5 percent a year, just 2 percent higher than the public library's.

The 30 percent figure was helped in the beginning by one young girl who came in every Monday afternoon and stuffed a dozen or so books into an old brown paper bag, titles ranging from James Baldwin's *Tell Me How Long the Train's Been Gone* to *The Three Little Pigs*. Every Friday she returned them. By the fourth week I couldn't contain my curiosity any longer, and I asked her what she did with all of them. She grinned, and explained that the Baldwin-type books went to her mother, the nursery books to her younger brothers, and the in-between books to anybody in the neighborhood who wanted to read them. A branch library, as it were.

The library, of course, contributed significantly to my students' remarkable gain in reading ability. If children are close to what they consider good books, they will read them. But it seems that the farther away from the books they get—the school library, the public library—the less likelihood there is that they will be checked out. Also, a classroom library has unique advantages over a public library. When a very popular movie comes to town which the children can't get into, or for which they don't have the admission price, I purchase ten or twenty copies of the paperback. *Change of Mind* ("A

White Man's Brain Is Transplanted Into a Black Man's Body!") and *Scream and Scream Again,* a monstrous horror story, were runaway hits in my room last year. Most public (or school) libraries, even if they were allowed to stack the types of books kids want to read, couldn't get them as quickly.

Aside from the Monday-Wednesday-Friday afterschool program, I conduct quarterly "faculty meetings" for the student-teachers of my reading groups. They come in, grab an agenda and a Coke, and sit down to discuss any problem they may have with either their students, the quality of the books, or anything else that relates to the reading program. These meetings are eagerly awaited. At first, it was probably just curiosity as to what happens at a faculty meeting, later because it made the children feel important (plus they like free Coke). At one meeting I even had a student-teacher who had been absent for the regular school day. He appeared punctually at 3:05, an ironic sense of responsibility.

All these afterschool and weekend activities are fine for a teacher who doesn't have the responsibility of another job or a family of his own. But even these nine-to-three teachers can see their students out of school. It's as easy as taking them to lunch. On the 73-second formula, a 45-minute lunch period with a student is the equivalent of seeing him in class for two months.

6

"DO YOU LIKE MY PAINTING?"

Timothy had stayed behind after class. He approached me slowly, pulling his painting out from between the sheets of an old newspaper. He thrust the painting into my hands, then quickly stepped back.

"Do you like it?"

At the Beach was a paint-by-numbers portrait of a young girl in a bikini. What I saw first was a badly soiled canvas with splotches of color. As I began to examine it, the uncertain artist edged closer.

Suddenly, his hand shot out, trying to take the painting back before I could offer an opinion. Defensively he asked me again:

"Do you like it? Do you like my painting?"

I hesitated. . . .

Some ghetto teachers would have compared *At the Beach* with Botticelli's *Birth of Venus*. "Timothy, this is the most beautiful thing that I've ever seen in my life." Then they would have returned it to him. Other teachers might have explained to him that the painting wasn't completely bad, for a child, and they would have added that he might consider devoting as much energy to his schoolwork. Either reaction would have confirmed Timothy's suspicion that he had failed—again.

Ghetto students, for the most part, are convinced that they are "no good, stupid, dumb." They have heard it from almost all of their teachers from the first grade on:

> "You're doing it wrong."
> "Can't you understand anything?"
> "What do you mean you don't 'get it'? It's written right on the page."

But I don't think the majority of teachers intentionally promote their students' feeling of failure. Their acts of degradation are more of a response to the pressures inherent in trying to teach in a slum school. Urban teachers watch their students fall farther behind, month after month, year after year. Eventually, if only quasi-consciously, the teacher must ask himself why. What causes his students to fail?

In answering this sensed-but-unspoken question, the ghetto teacher has a choice. His students fail either because (*a*) he is a bad teacher (and therefore a failure himself) or (*b*) for any of several possible reasons, his students are "unteachable." Faced with this dilemma, the teacher will save his own self-image by asserting that his pupils cannot be taught (an idea quite originally

presented in George Leonard's *Education and Ecstasy,*
Delacorte Press, 1968). They are "unteachable" because
their homelife is so poor, or because their former teachers
didn't adequately prepare them, or because the entire
school system is inferior, or because. . . . "How can you
expect me to build a second story," the ghetto school
teacher asks in psychic self-preservation, "when the
building doesn't have a firm foundation?" Or, in the
privacy of the men's faculty room he will be more blunt:
"You can't make chicken salad out of chicken shit. These
kids are nothing but dumb animals."

There are additional reasons for the urban teacher's
incessant criticism of his students. One is lack of patience,
certainly one of my worst shortcomings initially:

> "Please number your answers consecutively
> along the left-hand margin.
> "Yes, on the side with the red line on it."
> (Annoyed): "No, consecutive means one after
> another.
> (Angry): "No, you cannot skip a line between
> numbers.
> (Angrier): "Yes, one number right after an-
> other! Don't you listen?"
> (Furious): "One after another! One after
> another! Can't you even number a page cor-
> rectly?"

It isn't necessary to have Job-like patience, but, as I
learned, there is no advantage in being a scholastic Ster-
ling Moss—the students will be left behind.

There are, finally, two other reasons why urban teachers deprecate their students. They are racial in scope, and both black and white teachers are equally at fault.

Many white teachers make no effort to understand their black students' world. Other white teachers make only a halfhearted attempt, and erroneously conclude that the black child's culture is not different, but inferior. In a perverse way, these teachers expect poor performance from their students. When the prophecy is fulfilled they are disappointed but not surprised, for "what can you expect from kids with such a terrible background?"

In contrast, there are some teachers who know their pupils' world intimately. They are black, have struggled out of the ghetto, and have selflessly returned to teach in it. Many times, unfortunately, this black teacher sets unrealistically high standards for his students. He forgets that he was one of the few who made it out of the slums, and he cannot understand why they won't try to do the same. When his students don't immediately meet his expectations—it takes time to shuck off ten or fifteen years of failure—this black teacher becomes impatient and begins to criticize his students in the same ways as his white colleagues.

Psychic self-preservation, impatience, many prejudicial white teachers, some unrealistic black teachers—all cause the ghetto student to see himself in his better moments as incapable, in his worse moments as incurably incompetent. But this same student *can* change. And it is important that he does, because self-esteem forms the base of any person's pyramid of attitudes and values. If a child sees himself as without worth, he won't be overly involved in personal feelings of honesty, trust, or respect.

Nor will he make any effort to advance himself academically. (The opposite is also true, of course, so that
the twin goals of my program—reading and raising a
student's feeling of self-image tend to enhance each other.
A child who can read has a 100 percent better chance of
regarding himself in a positive way than a child who
cannot.)

Initiating the transformation of the way a child views
himself is not as difficult as it might seem. First, the
teacher must stop degrading the child. Second, as this
occurs, he will have an increased opportunity to give
this child the active encouragement he needs. At the
outset, then, it isn't as important to do something positive for the ghetto student as it is to stop doing things that
are negative. Even in the most difficult of situations,
maintaining classroom order, the urban teacher need
not be negative.

The pencil lands in the front of the room. What does
the teacher do now? Haim Ginott, in *Between Parent
and Child* (Avon Books, 1969), suggests a criticism not of
the child, but of the child's behavior. "What's-wrong-with-
you-didn't-you-hear-me-say-you-can't-throw-pencils?" at-
tacks the student's personality (and will provoke his re-
taliation, causing further trouble). On the other hand,
"Throwing pencils is against the rules of my room" only
shows the child that his conduct is inappropriate (not
feeling personally threatened, he won't be forced to de-
fend himself). This "nonnegative" criticism is more than
a technique; however, it's the teacher's attitude that the
child's feelings come first. Each time a child in my room
breaks a game, for instance, I try to contain myself long

enough to ask which is more important, a replaceable
$3.50 game or an irreplaceable child?

In addition to a change in attitude, most ghetto teachers need to change their materials. Forcing a child to
attempt work beyond his capacity assures failure—in
both the work and the child. The U.S. map in the beginning of the book is a good example of this. If the
teacher really wants to have his students learn map-
making skills, he should try having them do a map of
the gang territories in the school's immediate area (such
as the one on page 93).

The teacher who stops degrading his students will begin to notice them "do something right." At this time
he can offer the encouragement needed to build their
confidence.

The best method I've found for creating self-esteem
is to let my students, to the fullest possible degree, run
the class. Aside from the fact that they will teach and
lead one another better than I can, they feel trusted, important, and worthy of respect. The story of Ricky Ad-
derly, which occurred during the year I used formal
grouped reading, serves as an example.

Ricky was a quiet, guarded boy. During the first few
months of school he hardly said a word. His chance to
teach a group came in the middle of the year, but he
was hesitant to accept it. After much cajoling on my
part, though, he agreed to take it on a trial basis.

He started out badly, unsure of himself. He couldn't
control the constant bickering of the three members of
his group. Each day their squabbling got louder, yet
Ricky did nothing. The situation finally reached a climax

at about the group's tenth meeting. They were having
another of their frequent arguments—this time about
who was to read next:

> "You don't read next, I do."
> (Loud): "No, you don't, I do."

Ricky sat silently.

> (Louder): "You do not!"
> (Louder): "I do, too!"

By this time they were so boisterous that the rest of
the class had turned around to watch. They awaited
the outcome.

> (Yelling): *"YOU DO NOT!"*
> (Screaming back): *"I DO, TOO!"*

Ricky, humiliated to the point of action, jumped up
and hollered:

> *"I'M THE TEACHER OF THIS HERE
> GROUP, AND I'M GONNA READ NEXT!"*

Whereupon he sat down and started to read. The rest
of the class, satisfied, drifted back to work.

Less than three weeks later, Ricky came in after school
and asked if he could take his reader home so that he
could "prepare my lesson for tomorrow."

Fostering responsibility is the urban teacher's best
method of raising student self-esteem. There is a mul-
titude of secondary methods and techniques.

Sending letters to, calling, and visiting parents to tell
them of their child's positive accomplishments make any
student feel proud (chances are that the last letter they
got from the school was a suspension notice).

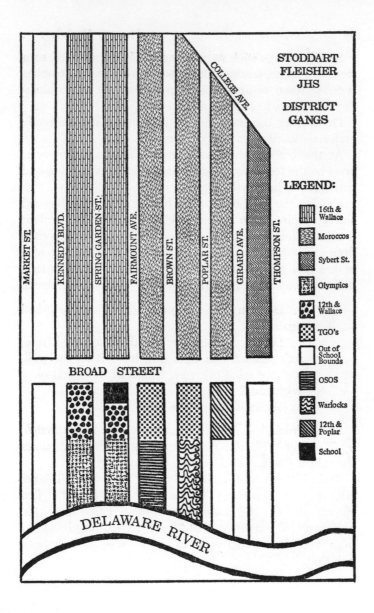

Simple things such as mailing a Christmas card to a student's home, sending him a postcard when the teacher is out of town, or presenting him a small gift on his birthday make him feel important.

Decorating the classroom with exciting, student-made materials instills a sense of competence.

At the core of these and similar methods, however, must be the teacher's vision of his students as capable and trustworthy human beings.

Finally, the teacher must be honest. The selective and sincere praise of an honest teacher can give the student a tremendous inner feeling of achievement. Ghetto children are not deceived by false flattery. The teacher who makes this superficial effort only tells his students in a different way what they already sense—they are failures.

> "Do you like my painting?" Timothy asked again.
>
> "I think so, but I really don't know. Listen, let's put a frame around it, hang it on the wall, and see what everyone thinks of it. Is that okay with you?"
>
> (A slight grin): "Uh-huh."

So we framed it and put it on the wall: *At the Beach*, by Timothy Williams. Without exception, his classmates thought it great. A real, framed oil painting!

Today there are eight original Timothy Williams' adorning my classroom. To me, most look like that first canvas, and I'm still not certain whether I like them. I'm not surprised, however, that Timothy's reading level has improved almost two years in the six months he's been painting.

7
"WHERE IT'S AT"

Joe the Janitor, a disgruntled man at best, is especially peeved two days each year. If you happen to pass my school on one of those two days, you'll see a freely-perspiring Joe, pressing his vibrating body against the sandblaster that in turn is pressed against an outside wall of the school. Joe is vainly attempting to erase the spray-painted and magic-markered initials, 1-2-P, M, 1-6-W, and the like. His task reminds me of the story of Sisyphus, a character in Greek mythology who had been condemned by the god Zeus to spend all eternity pushing a heavy boulder up a steep hill. At the instant he reached the summit, the boulder fell back to the bottom and he would have to start all over again. In much the same way, before Joe has finished the west wall of the school, the markings have reappeared on the south wall.

The initials are the trademarks of area gangs: 12th and Poplar Streets, perhaps the most vicious group of boys in Philadelphia; the Moroccos, their perennial rivals; 16th and Wallace; and so many other insignia that you begin to believe that there are more gangs than there are street numbers and letters to support them.

When I started teaching in North Philly, I regarded the gang activities as a sort of modified *West Side Story;* the kids couldn't sing too well, and who could take all that childish mumbo jumbo seriously? Today, four years later, gangs still seem to be childish foolishness, but I wouldn't compare them to a Broadway musical. It loses its humor when twenty or thirty eighth-grade students come to school one morning wearing black armbands, a temporary symbol of mourning for a fellow gang member who had been shot or stabbed to death the night before—temporary, because by that evening they will have retaliated, and the next morning there will be a different set of students bearing the black armbands.

In the area surrounding my school there are nine gangs. They are not flighty little groups of half a dozen youngsters. They are highly organized, fairly sophisticated combinations that number as high as 150 to 400 members. These gangs include youth of all ages, from the Peewees (six and under), through the Midgets, Juniors, Seniors, and Old Heads. Old Heads are over eighteen and are either high school dropouts or graduates.

The complexity of living in an area controlled by gangs is dizzying, whether you are a member or not. There are certain streets you can walk on, certain ones you can't. There are some avenues and alleys where you can go safely only if you're accompanied by a dozen friends, others where your life is endangered no matter how many allies are with you. Coming to school in the morning and leaving it in the afternoon is an adventure in terror that might have unnerved James Bond. (And it is a good part of the reason that the absentee rate in my school runs well over 20 percent, and some days reaches as high as 40 percent or 50 percent.) The map on page 99 is not unusual. The dash line shows the shortest distance for a student from home to school. The solid line shows the route he must take if he's going to have a better than even chance of making it at all.

The community-gang environment is one third of "Where It's At" for the urban child as a student. The other two thirds are the school itself and the individual classrooms of teachers.

Schools are usually considered neutral territory by the gangs, so that there is little open hostility in the building. The promises to have a "fair one" (one-on-one fist-fight, sometimes ends up fair, often doesn't) are made in the building but are carried out around the corner after three o'clock. The school, then, may be indirectly affected by the tensions in the neighborhood, but it is still independent of them to a large degree.

School, therefore—just the physical building itself—could be a colorful refuge from the drabness and anxiety of the area around it. But in the majority of cases it isn't. Most inner-city schools could be transformed into maximum-security prisons without many major modifications. The windows are already barred; the entrance doors—those which aren't always locked—are heavy metal; the interior of the building is painted—if it has been painted at all in the past fifteen years—with something that would make gunmetal gray look enticing; and most classrooms are already drab enough to pass for cellblocks. The only major change that would be necessary to convert the building would be to sweep the halls. Prisons, unlike schools, don't look like the "before" part of an advertisement for litter control.

In an effort to disguise the fantastic shabbiness of the place, bulletin boards are scattered around the walls. Until five years ago, these boards unanimously proclaimed the virtue of a balanced diet, clean fingernails, and homework. With the present stress on "relevance," however, only one half the boards call for bright teeth. The rest extol such men as Thurgood Marshall (first black Supreme Court Justice) and Frederick Douglass ("Father of Black Freedom"). All of which is fine for a month or two, but Marshall's legal secretary probably doesn't see him as often as these students see his picture. No surprise then that it only takes a day or two for the inevitable initials to appear, scrawled over Carl Stokes's (first black mayor of a major Northern city) moustache in red magic marker.

For some unfathomable reason, school administrators must want their schools to appear conformingly colorless, because it's so easy and inexpensive to make the place look exciting that it's almost more of an effort to leave it dull. One simple solution is construction paper and scotch tape. To wit: papering the walls in imaginative patterns, shapes, and designs. It could be done in an hour or two if all the kids took part. And having the students participate is one way to ensure that their markers will be reserved for somebody else's building. Today,

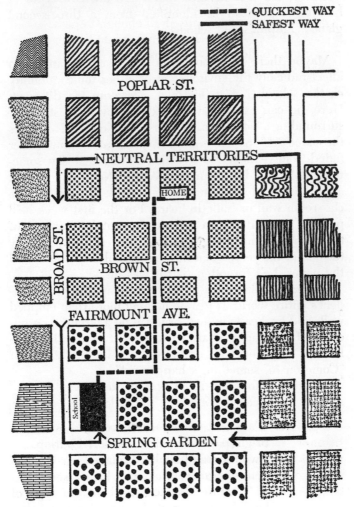

FROM HOME TO SCHOOL,
AVOIDING GANG TERRITORIES

- - - - QUICKEST WAY
———— SAFEST WAY

POPLAR ST.

NEUTRAL TERRITORIES

HOME

BROAD ST.

BROWN ST.

FAIRMOUNT AVE.

School

SPRING GARDEN

however, the fact remains that there are two types of buildings that can be identified from a three-second glance: hospitals and schools.

Maybe there isn't too much one teacher can do to affect radically the environment of either the community or the school, but in his own classroom it's different. Here, he can exert complete control over his students' surroundings. Too often, of course, he doesn't. He leaves the same "A" papers up for months at a time under faded-from-years-of-use stenciled letters that say something dynamic, like "Our Best Work." Now it's true that any child is pleased to have his work put up on the classroom wall or bulletin board. For the first week he'll proudly point it out to his friends. But by the end of the month he may begin to lose interest in it, and by the end of the year, when dust has completely obliterated the paper, he's forgotten that it was his.

A teacher's classroom is, however temporarily, his student's entire world. It can be nothing more than chipped walls and broken windows, or it can be a circus, a cornucopia of constantly changing colors. It can call out to him, in his world of drabness, and invitingly shout: "Come on in, something's happening!"

The day before my room was packed away for the summer last year it contained the following:

1. Walls that were partially covered over with bright panels of different-colored burlap.
2. Two thousand books, displayed in some student-designed brick and board shelves.
3. A "Feature" bookcase, where the type of book being promoted changed each week—

from romance stories one week to *Peanuts* the next.

4. The Reading Progress Board, which took up one entire wall.
5. A "What's News" Bulletin Board, the news changing at least once weekly.
6. Some framed student paintings, some student-sculptured African masks, and endless posters of "Black People Who Made It," such as the Temptations and the Royal Five (both singing groups).
7. A magazine rack that always had its share of comic books.
8. A huge glass cabinet filled with games and toys.
9. An electric organ ($29.95).
10. Four rubber trees and about twenty-five other plants.
11. Three fish tanks—two gold, one tropical.
12. Two gerbil cages, complete with gerbils.
13. A mouse cage.
14. Two hamsters.
15. Four turtles.
16. One ant farm.

Even if all these things were just piled in the corner, and not laid out with an eye-pleasing effort, they would have had to make my classroom a place where students wanted to spend time. This is a major accomplishment in and of itself, but is only one of the results I obtained by having made my room "Where It's At." (Each year I make up a different title for the room. The year before it was "It's What's Happening.")

Let's start with the animals. Even if it were possible for me to take care of the cleaning, watering, and feeding of some forty-five animals, I wouldn't. They are an excellent way to teach kids some of the social discipline that I mentioned in Chapter 1. At the beginning of the year, I give each group of animals to one or two students with the understanding that they can keep the animals, cages, and supplies at the end of the year if they agree to be totally responsible for them during the year. I have no trouble getting volunteers. And who would claim that bringing a carrot to school every day teaches less responsibility than bringing a pencil? (Of course, from the student's point of view, there's a reason to bring a carrot.)

The animals, as well as the plants and almost everything else in the room, teach children how to read. Taking care of, or merely watching, animals inevitably leads to questions: "Why does a turtle get a soft shell, and what can you do about it?" "Do the hamsters have to be taken home for the Christmas vacation, or can they get along on their own with enough food and water?" "How can you tell if a goldfish is pregnant?" These and other questions are answered in one of the countless "How to Take Care of Your —————" manuals that sits next to each cage. And sooner or later a student will have to read the manual. In the case of Jimmy Taliaferro, it was much later.

Jimmy was a rotund, always-smiling youngster with a very pleasant disposition. Though he had an average reading ability for students at my school, he had an absolute aversion to looking at a printed page. In December, I bought four mice, which Jimmy volunteered to care for. One day in January, as I walked into the room, I heard him call me:

> (Thrilled): "Mr. Daniels, Mr. Daniels, hey, the mice had babies! Look at those ugly pink things!"

"Say, that's really great. Be sure to give them more food."

In February:

> (Excited): "Hey, Mr. Daniels, the other ones had babies. There's gotta be fifteen mice in there now. How can I take care of them all?"

"Why don't you take a look at the mouse book?"

> Ignores comment, turns away to look at the mice.

Late March:

> (Perplexed): "Mr. Daniels, geez, there's about fifty mice in there now. It's getting so crowded. How can I stop it?"

"You could read up on it."

> Ignored.

Early May:

> (Angry): Hey, Mr. Daniels, if we don't stop this, there's gonna be a million mice in there pretty soon. You better tell me what to do."

"I'm not going to tell you anything. They're your mice. You've got a book that tells you what to do. Either read it or give your mice to somebody who will."

> He reads it.

P.S. This didn't turn out to be one of the world's great success stories. Jimmy read the manual thoroughly, separated the males and the females, and didn't read another word for the rest of the year. But better a mouse than nothing.

As well as being "alive," a room should have decorations that are constantly changing. Men landed on the moon in July, 1969. They left it in July, 1969. Moon decorations and displays landed in classrooms throughout the country in September, 1969. But many of them didn't leave until June, 1970. And nobody was looking at them after the first couple of weeks.

One way to keep the room changing is to have a new theme for each month, which doesn't necessitate pumpkins in October and turkeys in November, but could include "Famous People I'd Like to Date" month, or "Jobs I Wouldn't Mind Having" month. Unfortunately, I found that this suggestion reads better than it is. Each month for a couple of years I completely changed the room decor (with the help of the kids). The decorations were stimulating and attractive, but they were also so time-consuming to think up, put up, and tear down that I came to resent the end of each month. Eventually, I hit on a compromise solution, one that required less work, but which kept the classroom looking new and lively.

At the beginning of the year my students help set up permanent "displays." Then, each week during the year, I change what's in them. Thus the featured "Book of the Week"; "Record of the Week"; "Game of the Week"; new magazines in the old rack; the Reading Progress Board, which itself remains stationary but on which the students' flags are continually moving; and so forth. The plants and animals, of course, add to the atmosphere of "newness."

Finally, in addition to being alive and constantly changing, classroom decorations must make sense to the students. This is so obvious that it doesn't require elaboration, but those same teachers who continue to use eighth-grade textbooks with third-grade readers skimpily decorate their rooms with "Our Best Work."

Would you rather sit in a classroom that was decorated with:

> a. An "A" paper that proves that a student has the capacity to memorize ten science terms he doesn't understand
>
> or
>
> b. A large corner that, with wire mesh and wood, has been built into a cage for bunny rabbits?

> a. A perfectly executed map of Oregon made by a student in a Boston social studies class
>
> or
>
> b. A map of the district of the school with a picture of each student glued to the block he lives on?

> a. An English essay about "What I Did During My Christmas Vacation"
>
> or
>
> b. Twenty copies of *Black Like Me* (Signet), which, if you're interested, you may take home to read?

8

THE PARENTS

Do the parents (aunts, uncles, grandparents, guardians) of ghetto children care about either their children or the school their children attend? If they do, why don't they demonstrate it by coming to the Home and School Association meetings? Why don't they reply to a teacher's request that they come to school when their child is in trouble?

The first question, Do they care about their offspring? is rhetorical. If, after six or twelve years they don't, there is very little anyone can do to change their mind. Human nature being something of a constant, though, ghetto parents are probably no different in this respect from suburban parents. Some love their children and some are indifferent. But you'd lose money if you bet that a student could come home from a junior high school in Shaker Heights with all "F's" and find his parents didn't even call the school to discover why. Or that only one percent of the parents at Beverly Hills High would attend a P.T.A. meeting. If it's true that ghetto and suburban parents feel the same way about their children, why are their reactions to their children's school so different?

First, there are the practical reasons. When a mother works all day, she really doesn't want to walk through dangerous gang territory to get to school at night. She can't come between nine and three because it would mean the loss of a day's pay, and therefore less food for the family. In other cases, a mother is often divorced or separated and the only parent her children have. If there are babies in the house, she can't leave them alone. Hiring a sitter is out of the question.

In addition to these and other pragmatic reasons that keep parents from the school, there are many psychological ones. First, these parents remember school from their own days, and the great majority of them disliked it. Second, many parents feel very insecure talking with teachers and administrators; they are embarrassed to show their own lack of education (and many condescending school personnel don't discourage this). Third, a small minority of very militant parents refuse to enter a building run by the "White Establishment." Common to these and other parents is their basic distrust of the school. They recall too well all the classroom lectures about an education being the only road to decent employment. Having either quit or finished, most discovered that they could find only menial positions, regardless of their scholastic background. National racial discrimination isn't entirely the schools' fault; glossing it over is.

The parents' ill will is tempered, however, by the
knowledge that the social system has changed since
they were in school; that today, perhaps, their children
can go to college and can make an honorable living. For
that reason most parents—though they won't enter the
school themselves—feel that their children need to go.
Unhappily, they won't find out for years that their dreams
for their sons and daughters are unrealistic. The school
system has not changed. Their children will most likely
end up as uneducated as they themselves are. Their false
hopes lead to scenes such as this one, which was
played out in my classroom a couple of years ago.

Janice Green had been suspended for fighting with
another girl in the cafeteria. Three days later, her
mother brought her back to school (under suspension,
a child may not return unless accompanied by a rela-
tive or guardian). Janice came up to the classroom
while Mrs. Green was lectured to by one of the school's
administrators. A few minutes later, furious, Mrs. Green
rushed into the room, and, without talking to anyone,
ran over to her daughter, picked her up by the neck,
dragged her in front of her classmates, and started ad-
ministering a terribly severe beating. She slapped her
hand across Janice's mouth, crying out:

> "You gotta stop messin' 'round, and get your-
> self an education." (Slap.)
>
> "You gotta get yourself educated, child."
> (Slap.)
>
> "You ain't gonna end up like me, sweeping
> the floors." (Slap.)
>
> "You're gonna mind your teachers, and get
> yourself an education!" (Slap.)

Many blows later, she stopped. She pushed Janice away from her, apologized to me for the interruption, and, shoulders bent over, left the room. Her tears didn't show. Her daughter's did.

What is criminal is not that Mrs. Green slapped her daughter. It's that all the slapping in the world won't make Janice Green educated. Her mother, barely able to read, cannot teach her, and the school only feigns the effort to communicate with her what it's doing to/for her daughter.

A principal would vehemently object to the word "feigns." He would tell me that he's aware of all the reasons I've outlined that explain parents' uninvolvement with his school, that he realizes that effective education is dependent to a degree on close ties between home and school, and that he is doing everything possible to change their attitudes. Then he would pull a file out of his cabinet and tell me that he has sent home (via the forgetful children) seventeen letters to parents, inviting them in, reminding them that he is there to serve them. Typical of his letters is this one, which introduces a new newsletter:

Dear Parents:

This monthly newsletter represents a very important step in extending the lines of communication between our school and the community. In our community report we shall attempt to present a complete account of our school's activities so that the community is fully apprised of the nature and extent of our program.

It is our hope that this newssheet will in addition contribute to greater concern and involvement of

our community in the life of the school, so that our
curriculum may more effectively be related and
responsive to the needs of our youngsters and the
desires of our community.

I am sure that this relationship can be established
and extended. May I therefore request your reactions to and suggestions for our monthly report?

Sincerely yours,

So the parent—or those few who might possibly understand the language in this letter—is left with an uneasy
feeling about school.

What all this should indicate to the individual teacher
is that he can expect almost no voluntary help from the
home, and often no help even when he asks for it. In
concrete terms, this means that his calls home about a
student's misbehavior may be ignored, that parents won't
contribute any materials to his classroom (see the next
chapter), and that his program, whatever its nature, will
not be reinforced at home.

Since this naturally works the other way, too, it's as-
suredly to a teacher's advantage (and his student's benefit) to develop some sort of relationship with the parents.
Nor can he do this by waiting for them to come to him.
At least it didn't work for me this way.

My first experience with parents came on the annual
Open School Night during my first year. I had spent the
afternoon cleaning the classroom and decorating it
enough so that it looked respectable. (Room decor was
the farthest thing from my mind that first year, I had too
many other problems.) Then, trained by years of attending private school, I sat down to await the hordes
of parents who would come to discuss their children's

progress. In retrospect, of course, I'm not surprised that I spent from 7 to 10 P.M. in the room and saw a total of the older sister of one of my better students. (After my second Open School Night, I realized that it was usually the parents of the better students who came, which is probably one reason that their children were the better students.)

During my three-hour vigil that night—after getting over the initial shock of being quite alone—I began to develop techniques that eventually brought me close to my student's parents. My techniques have worked for some teachers I know, but not for others. This leads me to believe that central to any success with parents, and more important than any particular method, is a teacher's true concern for his students. If he really doesn't care about them, his efforts with their parents will look something like a machine-stamped car fender: perfectly executed, but notably lacking in feeling. If he is involved, the parents of his students may receive a letter like this one:

Dear Parents of 7-2:

Through some good luck, I have gotten a copy of the movie, *The Hustler*, which will be loaned to me on Saturday, February 8th.

I have invited, along with my wife Patty, the members of 7-2 to come to my home on Saturday to see the film, which stars Paul Newman and Jackie Gleason.

The movie will start at about 1:30, and the children should be home before it gets dark. [Here I listed my address and phone number].

Refreshments will be served.

Please tear off the bottom of this sheet and send it to me if your child has your permission to come.

Sincerely yours,

This type of letter is certain to get home with "the forgetful children." The next one should be mailed home.

To the Parents of _____:

The purpose of this letter is to let you know how your child is doing in my class at school.

This isn't a report card, and it does not go in the student's permanent record. But it does give me the chance to tell you how your child is doing in my class.

Somehow, today, the school and the parents don't get together enough. If you have any questions about this report, or about your child's work, I will be happy to meet with you at any time.

SUBJECT WORK
Excellent _____
Good _____
Fair _____
Poor _____

EFFORT
Tries hard all the time _____
Tries hard most of the time _____
Tries about half the time _____
Does not try at all _____

BEHAVIOR
Excellent _____
Good _____
Fair _____
Poor _____

OTHER COMMENTS ABOUT THE STUDENT'S WORK

I hope that you will get in touch with me if you have any questions. My phone number at school (from 9 A.M. to about 4 P.M.) is _____. My phone number at home (from 5 P.M. to 8 P.M.) is _____.

Sincerely yours,

This interim report was enthusiastically received. To begin with, it's much clearer than the Board of Education-issued report cards, which contain grades for something as fuzzy as "work habits." Work Habits is a category that, defying definition, most teachers use to express their personal prejudices: does the child bring a pencil to school every day (or a carrot, as the case may be)? This is fine for teachers, but it doesn't tell the parent anything. Also, a parent can't talk back to a Board of Education report card as easily as he can to my report. To question the formal one, he must come to school. To discuss mine, all he has to do is call me, which is much less threatening than a visit to the school. During the week after I mailed these, I received over twenty-five calls—all but one of them at home. And in this case I heard mostly from the parents of those children who were "poor, does not try at all." These interim reports, by the way, aren't as time-consuming to make up and send out as it might seem. I have the students fill their names in on the top of the page, and then address and stamp the envelopes.

Two months after the home-made report cards, I mailed this letter home:

Dear Parents of 7-10:

In my last letter, I mentioned to you that somehow the school and the home don't get together as much as they should. For that reason, I would like to invite you to Room 407's PARENTS WEEK.

The students of 7-10 join me in asking you to watch your child in my class during the week of March 24th to March 28th. 7-10 will be in Room 407 during these times:

Monday, March 24th................12:10–12:50
Tuesday, March 25th.................9:15–10:00
Wednesday, March 26th.............12:10–12:50
Thursday, March 27th..............12:50– 1:30
Friday, March 28th.................10:00–10:40

We'd love to have you come in. If you can't come in at these times, come in any time, and I'll be happy to talk with you about your child. Remember that if there's anything I can do for you, call me either at school (_____) or at home (_____).

                                    Sincerely yours,

The response was overwhelming. During the same year when only 11 of 1300 parents came to Open School Night, 20 out of 150 parents came to 407's Parents Week. They came in part because it was an invitation extended to them both personally and in readable English, and because by that time many of them knew me. If they hadn't met me on one of my neighborhood walks, they at least knew me indirectly; either through cards and letters I had sent their children when I was away on summer vacation, or from the books their children took home from the classroom's lending library, or through one of my numerous phone calls home. (When I call about misconduct, I try to find at least one nice thing to say to a parent about his child. Also, I always call back a couple of weeks later to let them know if there's been any improvement.)

One of the mothers who stopped in during Parents Week was Mrs. Carter, whose daughter was one of my three students who could read at grade level. She happened to come in on Friday, when the kids were playing games. To say that she was pleased at what she saw would be the same as saying that children adhere to the BE COURTEOUS sign while they drive those electric bumper-cars. "What," she demanded to know, "is Cynthia doing playing What's My Line? It's bad enough she watches it on television, but she doesn't need to waste her time in school." In response, I pulled two chairs over to a corner of the room and asked Mrs. Carter to sit with me. Then I launched into an enthusiastic monologue about my program, and the role of games in it. I agreed with her that What's My Line? wasn't teaching Cynthia to read, as she was already an excellent reader, but I stressed that there were other things that games teach. Finally, I told Mrs. Carter that she was, of course, free to disagree with my methods; but I asked her, before she condemned them completely, to take a walk around the school. I asked her to decide whether her daughter was learning any less in my room than she would be elsewhere. She agreed to this experiment, and I asked Cynthia to escort her through the building. About fifteen minutes later, Cynthia returned alone, offering me the cryptic message that "my mother said she will see you later." I had visions of a long-drawn-out battle, and was afraid that Mrs. Carter might want to remove Cynthia from my class.

It was a week before I saw her again. On Friday, she came into the class with her daughter. Cynthia led her over to the games cabinet, and they spent the entire period playing checkers.

All my contacts with parents over the past couple of years have made me a sort of ombudsman between them and the school. "Mr. Daniels, I'm going to send Kevin down to his grandmother in the South, to get him away from all this gang warring. Will you tell the school for me?" "Marvin is going to the clinic with me tomorrow, so don't you mark him down cutting." "Can you talk with Sharon's English teacher and find out how come she gave Sharon such a low mark in behavior?" The calls at home have reached the point where I hear from parents of children I don't even teach.

It's unfortunate that this kind of buffer is needed, but until school administrators make an effort to assess accurately their community's wants and needs, it will be a necessary role. The real pity is that there is often nobody around who can play the part, with the result that the gap that separates the home and school becomes a chasm.

The parents of my students do care about their children's activities in school. And because they do, they make my job both easier and more effective. And satisfying:

Dear Mr. Daniels:

Wayne went downtown to the store yesterday

and purchased the items he needs for the hamster. He wants to make sure you know that he has everything. And I want you to know that it is mighty nice of you to see that he has every possible means of enjoying the animal. I think he will never forget a teacher as nice or as thoughtful as you.

Thanks for everything,

9

TEACHING
ON $2.00 A DAY

There are many things that money doesn't grow on. Trees are one of them. Schools are a close second.

Gerbils, those tiny squirrel-like kangaroo rats, cost $3.95. Two thousand books cost about $1,500. And the supplies and other materials in between ran another $1,500.00 plus. Over a four-year period, my total expenditures have come close to $4,000.00. I happened to be lucky enough to have sold a few magazine articles that paid for some of these supplies, but this is as insecure a method of raising money as trying to catch fish without a worm; an occasional ignorant carp may hook himself, but hardly on a regular basis. The remainder of the money and materials for my classroom has been contributed.

My program, it's true, is somewhat expensive. There are undoubtedly other fine ways to teach ghetto students how to read, but no approach will be entirely free of extra financial expenses. The teacher who wants to put together a meaningful program is going to have to find money somewhere.

It never ceases to surprise me that the School District of Philadelphia has an annual budget of around three hundred million dollars a year, and that it's impossible for me to requisition a roll of scotch tape from the office at my school. Not because the secretaries hoard it, but because they just don't have it. It strains credibility.

I've yet to research formally why three hundred million dollars can't be translated into a 19 cent roll of tape, but in macabre daydreams, I imagine the following sequence:

The city, state, and national governments give the School District money. The School District, after keeping almost all of it for teacher salaries, management, and administrative expenses, parcels out the balance to the eight districts. Perhaps each district gets as much as one million.

The district, after lopping off their administrative costs, passes what's left to the approximately thirty schools in their area. Given that my principal gets along with the district superintendent, our school may get as much as $30,000.00.

After the principal takes his cut (for programs the district superintendent tells him to run), he calls a meeting of the department chairmen to discuss how they should divvy up the $15,000.00 that remains. Ten thousand dollars off the top goes to the science department, because they're building a new lab. The remaining $5,000.00 is allocated in such a way that the social studies department chairman gets $650.00.

The department chairman buys a slide projector and two tape recorders, then calls a meeting of the social studies teachers to distribute the what is now $350.00. This year there are eight social studies teachers. Each gets $43.75. Assuming full class loads, this means that each teacher can spend as much as 29 cents on each of his students for the year. That's if he can get the $43.75, which he can't. They don't give you the money in something as simple as cash. Rather, it's in the form of a credit with the Requisitions Department at the Board. Requisitions is the maze that Theseus practiced in before he went into the labyrinth to slay the Minotaur. Enough of the nightmare.

There are, as there would have to be, other ways to raise funds. Instead of waiting for the money to dribble down to him, a teacher can seize the initiative and, attired in knight's armor, can attack the Board personally. The School District of Philadelphia is unique in one respect: they provide a forum in which the Quixotes can battle their windmills. It is called Individual Teacher Grants for Innovation. Once a year any teacher in the system can submit a proposal with a request for funding up to $300.00. Apparently, mine is not the only school where scotch tape is unavailable. There are usually at least four hundred applicants for one hundred grants.

The first year I submitted for the grant I was rejected. As well as the second year. The third year I submitted the same proposal as I had turned in the second year. And was rejected again. The fourth year, using the same proposal I'd submitted twice previously, I was funded. What I've failed to mention, of course, is that by the fourth year I personally knew the man who supervised the Grants Committee.

Again, Philadelphia is singular. To the best of my knowledge, most large school systems have no provision at all for helping an individual teacher.

When he's given up trying to get any assistance from his home territory, the urban teacher can turn, as I did, to private industry.

Working in a ghetto school gives the teacher one great advantage: he can appeal to guilt-laden liberal organizations. The easiest way to do this is to write an appropriate variation of what I call my "Slum School Letter." In part, it reads: "I am sure that _____ [ten gallons of paint, twelve free tickets to a show, a fish tank, or whatever is needed] will have a profound effect on the children I teach. You can't begin to realize how grateful both they and I would be for your contribution to their education." And so on. (All organizations, of course, are not feeling remorseful about our country's present social situation, and some of the greatest help I've received has been from firms who are already deeply committed to urban education.)

Appealing to private industry is worth a teacher's time and trouble if he plans his approach intelligently. Asking for favors from publicly held corporations is almost more of an effort than their contribution will justify. An example: At one point in my search for materials, I wrote to the manager of a bank near my school, asking him to do-

nate some money to my classroom. After giving him a
week to look over my proposal, I called him. He was
sorry, he said, but he wasn't in a position to act on my
request. He had, therefore, sent my proposal downtown
to the central office. Would I call the assistant treasurer
there? I thanked the manager very much, gave the assistant treasurer a week, then called him. The assistant treasurer was out of town, his secretary informed me, and
could I call him back in a few days? Which I did. He was
sorry, he said, but my request wasn't in his realm of responsibility, so he would pass it on to the treasurer. The
treasurer, naturally, was on vacation. Three weeks later, I
talked with him. He had, it turns out, given the proposal to
the secretary to the board of directors of the bank. I called
the secretary, who suggested that I call him back after
he'd had a chance to review it with the board. I mentioned that by this time I was planning to leave for
summer vacation. So much the better, he said; that would
give him enough time to go over it. Why don't I call
him in September? Which I will. But if I had spent my
time washing dishes for $1.60 an hour instead of writing
thank-you notes and making phone calls, I would probably have more money than I asked them for anyway.

Medium-size companies, where I can talk with the
president directly, have been my biggest contributors.
During the past years they have donated close to a thousand paperback books, subscriptions to a dozen magazines, a few commercial games, some plants, and a
couple of animal cages. As a dollar amount, they have
given me about 30 percent of what I needed.

Some of the other 70 percent can be brought in by the
kids, no matter how poor the neighborhood they live in.

Parents have contributed old typewriters, food for class trips, and a record player to my room. They also involuntarily contributed books when I ran my one and only Book Drive.

I thought that the idea behind the Book Drive was simple, yet brilliant. For each book that a student brought in, I would give him a ten-cent Hershey bar. The only rules governing the candy-for-books swap were that the books had to be theirs, in good condition, and easy enough for them to read. I wasn't paying off for a dog-eared copy of *The Brothers Karamazov*.

The drive was much too successful. By the end of the first week I had doubled the month's goal of 250 books. I also found, when I went through the books a little more carefully, that most of them belonged to the public library. Not to mention the two frantic calls I got from parents who suddenly discovered their encyclopedia sets missing.

There's another tactic that I've used to get free materials which has proved quite effective. I write to the sales director of various publishing firms and mention that I'm interested in any new releases that might appeal to ten-to twelve-year-old readers. I don't exactly lie to him, but I do manage to imply that I'm in a position to order books for the entire school. Some of the examination copies that arrive as a result of my letters are not too good, and occasionally I get an aggressive phone call from a local salesman who represents one of the houses. On balance, however, it works out well.

Once, trying to pick up free materials, I wrote to the marketing director of every major manufacturer of commercial games. I offered them the use of my classroom as a testing base if they would leave the games when they were finished experimenting. I didn't get any takers.

A last side note on free materials. Unless a teacher's taste runs to the extremely esoteric, I advise staying away from those $1.95 paperbacks which offer "Twelve Million and Three Things For Free." If the publisher knew the whereabouts of an organization that was handing out gold bars for the asking, he wouldn't be selling its address for two dollars. Instead, his book offers a wall poster displaying the hubcaps of vintage cars, a guide to snipe hunting in the Everglades (with a big reminder across the cover page to "Drink Florida Orange Juice"), and a population map of Butte, Montana.

An aggressive teacher can obtain as much as 50 percent to 60 percent of all the materials and money he needs from companies, the community, and samples. Unless he has a rich father or his uncle is superintendent of schools, he's going to have to put out the rest himself. An almost painless way to do this—with apologies to Arthur Frommer—is by "Teaching on $2.00 a Day."

Today, when a teacher's pay begins to approach the level where moonlighting becomes a choice, $10.00 a week is not unthinkable. Nor is it really $2.00 a day. To begin with, the $2.00 is tax-deductible (or if it isn't, I.R.S. has been especially kind to me for three years). In a 20 percent bracket, the $2.00 is really only $1.60. Also, the $2.00 is not subject to sales tax, if the school's tax-exempt number can be pried loose from the school treasurer. (They seem to have some dread fear of people running amuck with their number.) Finally, the $2.00 can purchase as much as $2.80 retail worth of material, as almost

every store will give a humble and pleading school-
teacher at least a 10 percent and often as high as 30
percent discount. In all, then, $2.00 a day means that a
teacher can buy up to $2.80 worth of material for $1.60.
Not a bad deal.

Specifically, $2.00 a day buys one of those small Wool-
worth-type electric organs in three weeks. Or those
twenty copies of *Black Like Me* in six days. A typewriter,
and not one of those plastic models, in just a month. The
entire set of 125 Classics Illustrated Junior Comic Books
in nine days. After a few months, a teacher will have the
start of what will become an exciting classroom. A couple
of years of $2.00 a day guarantees that his room will
look like a cross between a library and an amusement
park—just the right balance for a stimulating educational environment.

It speaks poorly of centralized bureaucracy that the
only way a teacher can get many of the materials he
needs for his students is to buy them himself, but as of
today that's "the way it is." With a little imagination, it
needn't be that way tomorrow. Is there any realistic—
not pessimistic—reason why the following plan couldn't
be adopted by school boards?

Let's say that when I renew my contract with the
School District next year, I am given an account number
with the new Teacher's Materials Department (which
has replaced the old Requisitions Department). In that
account is $500.00. During the coming school year I am
free to spend this money on any materials I feel to be
appropriate for my students. The Board of Education,
through it's enormous purchasing power, has provided a
list of two hundred or so local "approved" stores where

I can purchase these items at large discounts. If there's a special item that I want which is not available at any of the listed firms, all I have to do is call downtown and Teacher's Materials will okay the purchase for me.

In early November, I decide that it's important to have a movie projector. First, I consult my school's Materials Center to see if any departing teacher left a projector. I find that no one has, so I consult my approved stores list and choose the one that I want to do business with. I go to that store to make my purchase. After selecting the model I want, the store writes down my account number, wraps up the projector, and I take it to my classroom the next day. (In the past, of course, I would have had to wait at least a few months for Requisitions to have it delivered to me.)

The store then takes the bill of sale and sends it, along with my authorization for the purchase, to Teacher's Materials. Materials issues the store a check the same week. (In the past many firms wouldn't do business with the Board no matter how large the purchase, because it used to take them months, sometimes years, to get paid.)

Under this new system, I get a quarterly statement from the Board—not dissimilar to the monthly statement I get from my bank—which tells me how much I have left in my account. If I had overdrawn my balance for the year, there would be a notation that the funds due the Board would be taken out of my next paycheck. At the end of the year any money I had remaining in my account would be added to my next year's $500.00. If I quit the system, any money left in my account would revert to the Board's general operating fund.

Careful consideration of this plan will show that it is

only disadvantageous to textbook publishers who sell
on a system-wide basis.

The plan would be remarkably effective for teachers.
A good teacher would be that much better if he could
order the materials of his choice. A not-so-good teacher
might be helped if he could obtain materials that he
would personally feel more confident using. In either
case, a teacher is the only school system representative
who comes in direct, full-time contact with his students.
Why should someone else order the materials he has to
teach with?

From the Board of Education's viewpoint, this plan
is both viable and a good deal better than what they
have now. It would save them thousands of man-hours of
work and enormous expense by eliminating at least:

1. Tons of requisitions forms, which are typed
   by school secretaries and read by secretaries
   at the Board.
2. All the proposals that teachers and administrators write to try to squeeze a few dollars
   out of the Board.
3. The myriad of paid consultants whose work
   consists of recommending the purchase of
   X instead of Y textbooks.
4. The entire Requisitions Department, and the
   middlemen who work for it. A Teacher's Materials Department could be staffed by four
   or five competent secretaries and a desk-
   model computer.

Finally, this kind of plan would probably cost less than
what the Board is already spending for materials on a

system-wide basis. While operating budgets make Hindustani easy reading by contrast, and it is difficult to make a penny-by-penny comparison, the present salary of the Director of Requisitions alone would fund about fifty teachers for a year.

Adoption of this kind of plan might even help educate children.

10

WHAT WILL BECOME OF JACKIE LEWIS?

If I had the three wishes that the fairy tales always offer the children, I would spend two of them to meet each of the students I've taught ten years from now. I'd like to know what will happen to them, whether I gave them enough in a year or two so that there will still be something left after the educational system tries to tear them apart.

Sometimes I sit and daydream, and wonder what will become of a young girl like Jackie Lewis. A pert, bouncy seventh-grader, Jackie wore her hair in a lovely round "Afro," always dressed in shouting colors, a yellow and purple cotton jumper print, underneath it a white sweatshirt reading "Here Come de Judge," or "Sock It To Me, Baby," a pair of white fishnet stockings, and the inevitable pair of black tennis sneakers. A girl "without a care in the world." Or so I thought until the

Monday I asked the kids to write a paragraph describing what it would feel like to be a piece of coal. She turned in this poem:

THE LITTLE PIECE OF COAL

I was a little piece of coal
Everytime the men came I got cold
It was a shame
How I got step on
As the men came through

People never notice me
As I got step on—

Now all my friends call me
Little Tom Coal
Who got step on

And I fear very much for Jackie's future. And for the future of all the Jackie Lewises. But then my daydreaming ends, and I am no longer sorrowful. Instead, I am angry.

I wonder when the bureaucracy will fulfill its obligation to Jackie Lewis. I wonder whether the people at the Board of Education realize that spending their time in headline-making political debates with local government and teachers unions does nothing for her. I question when they will understand that Jackie doesn't know that a new Deputy Superintendent for Innovative Curriculum was appointed two years ago, that for all the effect he's had on her, there's no reason she should. That anything he might attempt to do for her goes through so many levels that it's completely diluted by the time it reaches her.

But individual school administrators are all too well aware that this or that change has been made "downtown" at the Board. They know because even the most minor shift in policy or personnel is accompanied by three mailmen bearing pouches laden with new forms, applications, proposals, surveys, and requisitions "to be completed by all personnel and returned no later than Friday afternoon." And that this mania for forms is one reason why the principal of my school may not have the time to even meet Jackie Lewis.

A better-educated Jackie would tell me that these theoretical explanations of why she's getting no help are interesting, but what will they do for her? Telling her that people finally seem to be aware of her, that they at least appear to be trying to do something, and that maybe it will all work out a generation from now is an answer she wouldn't accept. What about tomorrow morning?

There is some hope for Jackie tomorrow morning. It can come from the same person who, not coincidentally, has the most influence on a ghetto student's education anyway. He is one of the people to whom I've directed this book: her teacher.

Jackie would interrupt me here. She would say, as she was accustomed to saying about many other things, that "it ain't fair." I would have to admit that she's right. It isn't fair that a teacher, as belabored as he already is, should have to compensate for the inefficiency, ineptness, and indifference of the Board of Education and many school administrators. But—these words should be mentally engraved—*he can do it.* And because he can, he should. Even disregarding the moral compulsion to right what is so tragically wrong, there is simply too much in it for a teacher to pass up.

First, almost too much satisfaction. The kind of gut-level joy that comes from being able to salvage a human life. It's not like the suburbs, where a good history teacher can influence a student to study law instead of medicine; it's watching a child go properly prepared for his first job interview knowing that if he had never met this or that teacher, he would most likely spend the rest of his life staring out of his housing project window.

All the biweekly paychecks from now till the millennium cannot match a teacher's inner knowledge that he, and he alone, is responsible for hundreds of lost children being able to read their first whole sentence.

And finally, that he is the teacher for whom Jackie Lewis wrote her poem.

If he doesn't care for either poetry or children, let him find a different kind of job. But if he does, I invite him to forget the people "downtown," to stuff the incomplete forms that are "due in the office no later than 10 A.M." in the bottom drawer of his desk, to take whatever suggestions of mine or anyone else's that he can use, and to join The Adventure!

11

"IT CAN
HAPPEN HERE!"

What follows are various suggestions for setting up a reading program similar to the one I devised. It's directed specifically to urban teachers.

In cases where I cite materials as being "best" or "most popular," I am—either through observation (games) or statistics (books)—measuring my student's attitudes toward the materials, not mine. I would personally find *The Children's Shakespeare* to be a "better" book than *Durango Street,* the story of a young man who joins a gang and gets in trouble with the police. But as a teacher, I must consider the latter to be "better," because it was read every day last year, whereas the Shakespeare was read only once. And there is no book less effectivo than one that isn't opened.

THE TEN BEST CLASSROOM GAMES
(in order of preference)

1. Checkers
2. Playing cards
3. Monopoly
4. The Game of Life
5. The Newlywed Game
6. Go to the Head of the Class
7. Ker-Plunk
8. Tip-it
9. Jigsaw puzzles
10. Spill and Spell

Coincidentally, the most popular games are the least expensive. Checkers and a board are 49 cents or less, and cards can be purchased for under half a dollar. A full set of the ten games would only take twelve days to buy—on $2.00 a day.

Whether the games should be strictly educational is a question I still can't answer. Initially, I stocked games that were only educational. Many of my students, however, found them pretty dull. So I put in things like Tip-it, which is essentially a balancing game. I don't think that Tip-it teaches as much as Parcheesi would, for example, but there are still many skills and attitudes that it does cover. It's an individual decision. I found that my children's enjoyment of the games carried over to everything else we did in class, which is sufficient for me.

I do advise staying away from games that require running around the room or violent physical contact, as they encourage control problems. This would apply to any game more active than Beat the Clock, for example.

You can't go wrong, by the way, picking up the games that are advertised on television. They always do well.

THE FIVE MOST POPULAR "GAMES DAY" MATERIALS

1. Electric organ ($29.95)
2. Typewriters
3. Tape recorder
4. Sewing machine
5. Erector-type sets

I buy these items as inexpensively as possible. They're going to be pounded constantly, and will probably break after a while no matter what their original quality. Anyway, why buy a $95.00 typewriter when you can get a new one each year for three years for the same money?

At the start of last year I bought forty LP's to go with the room's phonograph—records such as *William Tell* and *Robin Hood*. They were hardly ever listened to. On the other hand, friends of mine have found that their students really enjoyed them.

BOOKS IN THE READING LEVELS

The books that comprise the structured part of my reading program are arbitrarily divided into six levels of difficulty. The cutoff between levels is purposely fuzzy, and there is a lot of overlapping. I do this intentionally, to make my students feel more comfortable and confi-

dent. An example: a student has just finished the reading requirement for Level Two, and has gone over to
the Level Three bookcase to pick out his first book. If
Level Three is significantly more difficult, he may get
lost.

For the same reason, many of the books in different
levels are about the same people. Martin Luther King,
Jr., for instance, appears in Levels Two, Three, Four,
and Six. A student who is just starting in a new level,
then, can choose a subject that he is already familiar
with, which makes his transition an easier one.

I keep the levels physically separated as much as
possible to avoid congestion when the kids go to get
their books or to return them. When I started indi-
vidualizing my program I had the students come into
the room and sit as a class. Then I released them to
get their books. I thought that I'd dissuade any possible
misbehavior by calming them at the start of the period.
I found instead that it caused congestion near the book-
shelves and that it wasted ten minutes. A much better
solution, I discovered, is to have the children get their
books as they come in the door. There is usually a five-
minute period between the arrival of the first and last
students, so there is no crowding at the shelves. Also,
I find that this way permits me to retain order more
easily, as I can deal with one or two students at a time,
instead of an entire classful.

Each book in my levels has a "point value." This value
relates to the Reading Progress Board which was mentioned in Chapter 3. Last year, for example, the board
was a huge pegboard. Each student had his name listed
at the bottom of the board. Above his name was a peg.

To get to the top of the board, he had to get 96 points (each peghole was a point). The point value of the books was scaled in such a way that the payoff was for effort. In other words, a nonreader would get one full point for reading a Dr. Seuss book from Level One, whereas an excellent reader would collect only seventeen points for *The Autobiography of Malcolm X* in Level Six. In this way, even the worst readers in a class had an equal chance to get to the top of the board.

I updated the board once a month by going over my students' cards with them. Each student had a card in the room's file box. Every time he finished a book he went over to his card and entered the title, the level it came from, the number of points it was worth, and the date he finished reading it. I asked the students to write down the date so that I could keep cheating to a minimum. Since I didn't test them on the books, this was my only control. A student would have been hard pressed, for example, to claim that he'd read *Gone with the Wind* in four days.

The books, which are listed below by level, have been arranged by publisher, to facilitate ordering. Most of them are (or will shortly be) in paperback. Those which at present are not have an asterisk (*) next to the publisher. The books in each level which were the most popular are marked +. Books in which either black or Puerto Rican characters play a predominant or significant role are marked ×.

LEVEL ONE (0.1–1.5)

PUBLISHER	AUTHOR	TITLE
Golden Press*	Lowery and Carr	*Soft as a Bunny*
	Pierce	*Day of the Wind*
	Vogel	*Come On! Play Ball!*
Random House* (All of these are "I Can Read It All by Myself" Beginner Books)	Berenstain	*Bears' Picnic, The*
		Big Honey Hunt, The
		Bike Lesson, The
		Inside, Outside, Upside Down
	Cerf	*+Bennett Cerf's Book of Animal Riddles*
		+Bennett Cerf's Book of Laughs
		+Bennett Cerf's Book of Riddles
		+More Riddles
	Eastman	*Are You My Mother?*
		Go, Dog, Go!
		Sam and the Firefly
		Snow
	Elkin	*+King's Wish and Other Stories, The*
	Freeman	*You Will Go to the Moon*
	Gurney	*King, the Mice, and the Cheese, The*
	Heilbroner	*Robert the Rose Horse*
	LeSeig	*Come Over to My House*
		Eye Book, The
		I Wish That I Had Duck Feet
		Ten Apples Up on Top

PUBLISHER	AUTHOR	TITLE
	Lopshire	+*How to Make Flibbers Put Me in the Zoo*
	McClintock	*Fly Went By, A*
	Palmer	*Fish Out of Water, A*
		I Was Kissed by a Seal at the Zoo
		+*Why I Built the Booglehouse*
	Perkins	*Ear Book, The*
	Phleger	*Ann Can Fly*
		Whales Go By, The
	Seuss	*Cat in the Hat, The*
		Cat in the Hat Comes Back, The
		Dr. Seuss's ABC
		+*Green Eggs and Ham Hop on Pop*
		+*One Fish Two Fish Red Fish Blue Fish*
	Vinton	*Look Out for Pirates*
Viking	Keats	×+*Whistle for Willie*

To Progress to Level Two, You Must Read Any 20 of These Books.

LEVEL TWO (1.3–3.0)

PUBLISHER	AUTHOR	TITLE
Dell (Yearling)	Epstein	×*George Washington Carver*
	Graves	*John F. Kennedy*
	Patterson	×*Frederick Douglass*
Random House*	De Brunhoff, L.	*Babar Loses His Crown*

PUBLISHER	AUTHOR	TITLE
(Beginner)	Freeman	*You Will Go to the Moon*
	Holland	*Big Ball of String, A*
	Perkins	*Digging-est Dog, The*
		Don and Donna Go to Bat
		+*Hugh Lofting's Travels of Dr. Dolittle*
		+*Meet Chitty Chitty Bang Bang*
	Phleger	*You Will Live Under the Sea*
Random		*Meet Thomas Jefferson*
House*	Barrett	*Meet Abraham Lincoln*
(Step-Up	Cary	*Meet Andrew Jackson*
Level	DeKay	*Meet Christopher Columbus*
Books)		×+*Meet Martin Luther King*
		Meet Theodore Roosevelt
	Dyment	*Meet the Men Who Sailed the Seven Seas*
	Heilbroner	*Meet George Washington*
	Hornblow	+*Animals Do the Strangest Things*
		Birds Do the Strangest Things
		Fish Do the Strangest Things
		Insects Do the Strangest Things
	Payne	*Meet the North American Indians*

PUBLISHER	AUTHOR	TITLE
		Meet the Pilgrim Fathers
	Scarf	*Meet Benjamin Franklin*
	Trow	*Meet Robert E. Lee*
	White	+*Meet John F. Kennedy*
Random House*	De Brunhoff, J.	*Babar and Father Christmas*
		Babar and His Children
		Babar and Zephir
		Babar the King
		+*Story of Babar, The*
		Travels of Babar, The
	De Brunhoff, L.	*Babar and the Professor*
		Babar Comes to America
		Babar's Castle
		Babar's Cousin
		Babar's Fair
		Babar's Picnic

To Progress to Level Three, You Must Read Any 18 of These Books.

LEVEL THREE (2.6–4.5)

PUBLISHER	AUTHOR	TITLE
Archway (Washington Square Press)	Clayton	×+*Martin Luther King: Courageous Warrior*
	Faulkner	×+*Melindy's Medal*
	Gates	*Little Vic*
Dell (Yearling)	Beskow	*Astonishing Adventures of Patrick the Mouse, The*
	Burch	×*Skinny*
	Carlson	×*Empty Schoolhouse, The*
	Lofting	*Story of Dr. Dolittle, The*

PUBLISHER	AUTHOR	TITLE
	Stolz	*Bully of Barkham Street, The*
Follett*	Rose	×*Single Trail, A*
Harcourt, Brace*	Desbarats	×*Gabrielle and Selena*
Hastings House	Justus	×*New Boy in School, A*
		×*New Home for Billy, A*
Holt*	Hill	×*Evan's Corner*
Knopf*	Arnold	+*Brave Jimmy Stone*
Little Golden	Folk Tales	*Chicken Little*
		Pinocchio
		Three Little Pigs, The
		Winnie-the-Pooh
Morrow*	Friedman	×+*Ellen and the Gang*
Pantheon*	Coatsworth	×*Princess and the Lion, The*
	Fall	×*Eddie No-Name*
	Keats	×*John Henry*
	Neville	×*First and Last Annual Pet Parade, The*
	Parke	*Moon Ship, The*
	Weiner	×+*It's Wings That Make Birds Fly*
Platt & Munk*	Elkin (ill.)	+*Tell Me a Riddle*
Random House*	Barrie (Frank, ed.)	*Peter Pan* (abr.)
	Baum (Chaffee, ed.)	*Wizard of Oz, The* (abr.)
	Bourne	×*Raccoons Are for Loving*
	Davidson	*Pirate Book, The*
	Defoe (Frank, ed.)	*Robinson Crusoe* (abr.)
	Dolbier	+*Paul Bunyan*

PUBLISHER	AUTHOR	TITLE
	Farley	*Big Black Horse, The*
	Koral	*Abraham Lincoln* (abr.)
	(None)	*Stories That Never Grow Old*
	Salten (Chaffee, ed.)	*Bambi's Children* (abr.)
	Sewell (Vance, ed.)	*Black Beauty* (abr.)
	Spyri (Hayes, ed.)	*Heidi* (abr.)
	Van Leeuwen	×*Timothy's Flower*
Scholastic Book Service	Buff	+*Apple and the Arrow, The*
	Bulla	+*Sword in the Tree, The*
	Clymer	×+*My Brother Stevie*
	McGovern	*Aesop's Fables*
	Stone	*Pageboy of Camelot*
	Tralins	×*Runaway Slave: The Story of Harriet Tubman*
Signet	Fleming	*Chitty-Chitty-Bang-Bang*
	Neufeld	×*Edgar Allan*
Tempo	Bally	×*Hurricane Years: The Story of a Friendship*
Vanguard*	Seuss	+*And to Think That I Saw It on Mulberry Street*
		+*Five Hundred Hats of Bartholomew Cubbins, The*

To Progress to Level Four, You Must Read Any 15 of These Books.

LEVEL FOUR (4.0–5.5)

PUBLISHER	AUTHOR	TITLE
Archway (Washington Square Press)	Alcock	*Run, Westy, Run*
	Armer	*Screwball*
	Blanton	×+*Hold Fast to Your Dreams*
	Brodsky	×*House at 12 Rose Street, The*
	Edell	×*Present from Rosita, A*
	Graham	×*Story of Phillis Wheatley, The*
	Graham and Lipscomb	×*Dr. George Washington Carver: Scientist*
	Offit	*Soupbone*
	Schoor	*Jim Thorpe Story, The*
	Speevack	×*Spider Plant, The*
Avon	Hunter	×+*Soul Brothers and Sister Lou, The*
Bantam	Larrick (ed.)	×*On City Streets*
	Steinbeck	*Red Pony, The*
Dell (Yearling)	Alexander	*Black Cauldron, The*
	Jackson	×*Call Me Charley*
		×*Charley Starts from Scratch*
		×+*Tessie*
	Lenski	+*Cotton in My Sack*
		+*Judy's Journey*
		+*Strawberry Girl*
	Thompson	*That Barbara*
	White	+*Charlotte's Web*
		Stuart Little

PUBLISHER	AUTHOR	TITLE
Doubleday*	Sterling	×+*Mary Jane*
Harper & Row*	Neville	×*Seventeenth-Street Gang, The*
Knopf*	Baum	×*New Home for Theresa, A*
Lippincott*	Lenski	×+*High Rise Secret*
Popular Library	Barrett	×*Lilies of the Field*
Pyramid	Johnston	×*Soul City Downstairs*
Random House*	Dickens (Hastings, ed.)	*Oliver*
	Farley	*Black Stallion, The*
	Hitchcock	*Three Investigators Series (five titles in the series)*
	Keith	*Mutiny in the Time Machine*
Scholastic Book Service	Calhoun	*Depend on Katie John Katie John Really, Katie John!*
	Defoe	*Robinson Crusoe*
	Leeuw	*One Week of Danger*
	Peck	×*Martin Luther King*
	Sobol	*Secret Agents Four*
Signet	Graham	×*South Town*
Tempo	Salten	*Bambi*
	Shotwell	×*Roosevelt Grady*
	Stolz	×*Noonday Friends*
Viking*	Burch	×*Queenie Peavy*

To Progress to Level Five, You Must Read Any 10 of These Books.

LEVEL FIVE (5.5 AND UP)

PUBLISHER	AUTHOR	TITLE
Archway	Bawden	*Three on the Run*
	Robinson, Jr.	×*Arthur Ashe: Tennis Champion*
	Shapiro	×*Jackie Robinson of the Brooklyn Dodgers*
	Witton	×*Crossroads for Chela*
	Young	+*Where Tomorrow?*
Avon	Kaufman	×*Up the Down Staircase*
	Rodman	×*Lions in the Way*
Bantam	Adamson	*Born Free*
	Ball	×*In the Heat of the Night*
	Davis	×+*Anything for a Friend*
	Durham	×*Adventures of Negro Cowboys, The*
	Hilton	*Goodbye, Mr. Chips*
	Lipsyte	×+*Contender, The*
	Lord	*Night to Remember, A*
	Steinbeck	*Pearl, The*
Berkley	Harkins	*Day of the Drag Race, The*
	Newell	×*Cap for Mary Ellis, A*
		×*Mary Ellis, Student Nurse*
	Parks	×+*Choice of Weapons, A*
Coward-McCann*	Horowitz	×+*Diary of A.N., The*
Dell	Lester	×*To Be a Slave*
	Levin	*Rosemary's Baby*
Dell (Yearling)	Fall	×*Canalboat to Freedom*

PUBLISHER	AUTHOR	TITLE
	Fitzhugh	*Harriet the Spy*
		Long Secret, The
	Hoopes (ed.)	*Ali Baba and the Forty Thieves and Other Stories from the Arabian Nights*
	Jackson	×*Anchor Man*
	Sawyer	×*Year of Jubilo, The*
Doubleday*	Sterling	×*Freedom Train: The Story of Harriet Tubman*
Doubleday (Zenith Books)	McCarthy and Reddick	×*Worth Fighting For*
	Sterling and Quarles	×*Lift Every Voice*
Harper & Row*	Stolz	×*Wonderful, Terrible Time, A*
Pantheon*	Coatsworth	*Enchanted: An Incredible Tale, The*
Paperback Library	Soul Brother #44	×*Why We March*
Pocket Books	Bailey	×*Raw Pearl, The*
	David (ed.)	×*Growing Up Black*
	Gregory (with Lipsyte)	×+*Nigger*
Popular Library	Rock	×*Tick . . . Tick . . . Tick*
	Thompson	×*Nothing But a Man*
Prentice-Hall*	Meriwether	×+*Daddy Was a Number Runner*
Pyramid	Braithewhite	×+*To Sir, With Love*
	Cruz	×+*Run, Baby, Run*
Random House*	Nesbit	*Children's Shakespeare, The*

PUBLISHER	AUTHOR	TITLE
Scholastic Book	Bonham	×+*Durango Street*
Service	Lampman	*Shy Stegosaurus of Cricket Creek, The*
Scribner's	Hemingway	*Old Man and the Sea, The*
Signet	Evers	×*Sidney Poitier: The Long Journey*
	Huie	×*Three Lives for Mississippi*
	Thomas	×+*Down These Mean Streets*
Tempo	Hano	×*Willie Mays*
	Johnston	*Get Smart*
	Serling	*More Stories from The Twilight Zone*
	Sullivan	×*Wilt Chamberlain*
Viking*	Shotwell	×*Adam Bookout*
Westminster*	Newman	×*Marian Anderson: Lady from Philadelphia*

To Progress to Level Six, You Must Read Any 7 of These Books.

LEVEL SIX (7.0 AND UP)

PUBLISHER	AUTHOR	TITLE
Ace	Wright	×+*Long Dream, The*
Airmont	Stowe	×*Uncle Tom's Cabin*
	Verne	*20,000 Leagues Under the Sea*
Avon	Anderson	×*My Lord, What a Morning!*

PUBLISHER	AUTHOR	TITLE
	Corley	×*Siege*
	Hunter	×*Landlord, The*
	Joseph (ed.)	×*The Me Nobody Knows: Children's Voices from the Ghetto*
	Wright	×*Lawd Today*
Bantam	Boule	*Bridge Over the River Kwai, The*
	Gibson	*Miracle Worker, The*
	Keyes	*Flowers for Algernon*
	Kozol	×*Death at an Early Age*
	Walker	×*Jubilee*
Berkley	Eyerly	*Escape from Nowhere*
Dell	Baldwin	×*Another Country*
		×*Fire Next Time, The*
		×*Nobody Knows My Name*
	Cleaver	×*Soul on Ice*
	Hinton	×*Outsiders, The*
	Lopez	×*Afro-6*
Fawcett-Crest	Donovan	*PT-109*
	Parks	×+*Learning Tree, The*
	Puzo	*Godfather, The*
	Wallace	×*Man, The*
Grove	Malcolm X (with Alex Haley)	×+*Autobiography of Malcolm X, The*
Harcourt, Brace	Davies	*Miracle on Thirty-fourth Street*
	King*	×*My Life with Martin Luther King, Jr.*
Paperback Library	Johnson	×*Presidential Plot, The*

PUBLISHER	AUTHOR	TITLE
Perennial	Wright	×+*Black Boy* ×*Native Son*
Pocket Books	Christie	*And Then There Were None*
	Davis, Jr. and Boyar	×*Yes I Can*
	Mitchell	×*Gone with the Wind*
Pyramid	Orr	×*Black Athlete, The*
	Shea (ed.)	×*Black and the White, The*
	Wright	×*Eight Men*
Signet	Brown	×+*Manchild in the Promised Land*
	Ellison	×*Invisible Man*
	Griffin	×+*Black Like Me*
	Hansberry	×*Raisin in the Sun, A*
	Orwell	*Animal Farm* *1984*
	Williams	×*Man Who Cried I Am, The*
Tempo	Hass	×+*Troubled Summer, The*
World*	Halsell	×+*Soul Sister*

HOLIDAY GAMES

Playing a game with your students before a holiday is a wise thing to do for two reasons. First, you couldn't possibly conduct a regular class the day before Christmas vacation anyway, and second it gives you a chance to loosen up, to show the kids that you're not really a mean ogre.

One popular type of game is based on the kids' guessing the answer to some contrived question. At Christmas, for example, you can get a wall-poster Santa Claus for about a dollar. Then, buy a couple of rolls of cotton. Roll them up in a large ball, and attach them to Santa's beard. Then ask your students to write down the number of inches they think Santa's beard will extend after it's been unwound. Once you have their guesses, start the drama. You can dim the lights and shine a flashlight on the beard as a student slowly unrolls it. Every three or four inches you can stop to measure. Music in the background helps. Whoever is closest to the actual number of inches in the beard wins whatever the prize is. A reminder: if you teach more than one class, be sure to change the length of the beard for each of them. The word gets around pretty quickly that "it's 28 inches."

Another similar game is Halloween Screech. Lights dim. At the front of the room is a big, black cat with a wide-open mouth. At your side is a tape recorder with a taped screech. How many seconds?

There are countless variations of the guessing game. Most involve numbers and the action of a specific character. A different type of holiday game is based on skill. The Visual Turkey Hunt is one of these. The children enter a pitch-dark room. You explain that there are five chocolate turkeys hidden somewhere in the room. Then tell them that you'll turn the lights on for five seconds. Without leaving their seats, they must write down the location of one turkey (a well-decorated classroom helps camouflage the candy). If they do, they get it. If they don't, you can go to ten seconds, and so forth.

Of all the skill games I've used, my biggest success has been one that I used for Easter. Nobody seems to mind that it involves a lot of math, and the kids enjoy

moaning their way through a supercorny story. If you
have a pencil around, join in:

THE GREAT EASTER EGG CONTEST
OF 1970 PRESENTS
THE STORY OF STUPID STINKY
AND THE CHOCOLATE BUNNY

Once upon a time (which is the way all good stories
start), there was a young man named Stinky. Now all
his friends called Stinky, Stupid Stinky, because Stinky

was pretty Stupid. But I don't have the room here to
tell you why Stinky was stupid. You'll find out later.

Anyway, Stupid Stinky's mother told him to go to
town to buy their yearly Chocolate Bunny. His mother
gave him the five different-colored eggs you see in the
front of the room. As she gave them to him, Stupid
Stinky's mother told Stupid Stinky how much each egg
was worth. She said that the white egg was worth ten

cents, that the yellow egg was worth a quarter, that the pink egg was worth half a dollar, that the blue egg was worth a dollar, and that the green egg was worth a dollar and a half. Then she told Stupid Stinky that if he sold all the eggs for that much money, he would have a total of $3.35. Then she said to her son that the Chocolate Bunny would cost $2.50. She told Stinky that he could spend the 85 cents change on extra candy for himself.

So Stupid Stinky left the house and started for town. He kept all five eggs close to his stomach, for he didn't want anyone to steal them from him.

As Stupid Stinky was walking to town, he met an evil man by the name of Captain Getcha, who was always muttering to himself, "I'm gonna getcha." Captain Getcha asked Stinky where he was going with his pretty eggs. Stinky told the Captain that he was going to town. The Captain asked why. Stinky said he was going to sell his

five eggs and buy a Chocolate Bunny. "Well," said Captain Getcha, "I don't know if five eggs are enough to get a bunny." Stinky thought about this for a minute. He had forgotten what his mother had said about strangers. Then, Stinky said: "Geez, Mr. Captain Getcha, how can I get more eggs?" "Well," said Captain Getcha, "I'll trade you that pretty pink egg of yours for two of my eggs—one yellow and one white one." "That sounds like a great idea," said Stinky, and he traded. (Now you know why Stinky was called Stupid, or do you?)

So, now, Stinky had six eggs. Two white ones, two yellow ones, a blue one, and a green one. He continued to walk down the road, when all of a sudden he heard a scream coming from the side of the road.

"Oh, help me, help me!" screamed the voice. It sounded like a Princess in Distress, thought Stupid Stinky, so he ran to help her. When he got to the girl, he said: "Hello, I'm Stupid Stinky. Who are you?" "Boy," said the girl, "you must be pretty stupid. Why, I'm a Princess in Distress. Who else could I be?"

Just then, Stinky noticed an evil man who had the

THE
PRINCESS

Princess tied to a tree. "Who are you?" Stinky asked the man. "Boy," said the evil man, "you must be pretty stupid. I'm an evil man." "What are you doing with the Princess in Distress?" asked Stinky. "I'm holding her for ransom," the evil man replied. "How much do you want for her?" said Stupid Stinky. "Well, said the evil man, "I'll give you the Princess for one of those nice eggs." "Okay," said Stinky, "which one do you want?" "I'll take that blue one you've got in your left hand," said the evil man.

So Stinky gave away his blue egg. He had only five eggs left. But he also had a Princess in Distress. "Take me home," said the Princess, "and the King will reward you for saving me." "Okay," said Stinky, "where is your home?"

The Princess told him. It seems that you had to take the Broad Street subway to the end of the line, and then use a transfer to get to the King's Castle. Since Stinky didn't have any money, he had to pay both his and the Princess' subway fares with some of his eggs. Altogether, to get to the Castle cost him one of his yellow eggs.

The King was not very happy to meet Stupid Stinky. "Boy," said the King, "you must be kind of stupid." "How's that?" asked Stinky. "I didn't want my daughter back," said the King. "I'd paid to have her taken away. All she does is sit and watch television all the time, and I don't have enough money to pay the electric bills." "I certainly am sorry," said Stinky, "but the Princess said you'd give me a reward." "Well," said the King, "I guess it's not your fault you're so stupid," and he gave Stinky a pink egg.

On the way back to town (and he had to pay a white

egg to get the subway back), Stinky tried to figure out if he had enough money to buy the Chocolate Bunny his mother had sent him for. He couldn't add eggs very well, so he just went to the market and sold all the eggs he had. Then he counted up all his money, and he started to cry.

Stupid Stinky didn't have enough to buy his Chocolate Bunny. He knew his mother would be very angry. He didn't know what to do, so he just cried and cried.

Just then, a stranger walked by. He saw Stinky crying, and he asked him why. Stinky told him that he didn't have enough money for his bunny. The stranger said that he'd give Stinky the cash he needed. But since the stranger was a dentist, he said he wouldn't give Stinky enough to buy extra candy—just enough to buy the bunny. Which he did.

The stranger was happy. He was pleased because he knew that Stinky would get cavities from eating so much chocolate, and that Stinky would have to come to him to get his teeth fixed.

And Stupid Stinky was happy too. He walked home with his Chocolate Bunny, and his mother was very happy.

THE END

Question: (Without talking, bring your answer to the front of the room and check it with me): How much money did the stranger give Stupid Stinky so that Stinky could buy his Chocolate Bunny?

Answer: _____(If you played along, check your answer on the last page of this chapter.)

Returning from a vacation poses a problem. Too often a teacher makes no allowance for the natural transition that must take place between vacation play and school "work." The best kind of activity that I've found for the day right after a vacation is a story of some kind. It can be either entirely fun or lightly educational. Of all the stories I've used with kids, the ones that I write myself seem to evoke the greatest response. Either because I know the kinds of things my students like, or because they appreciate that "their teacher" wrote it.

BOOKS FOR THE CLASSROOM LENDING LIBRARY

The best way that I've found to stock a classroom lending library is to buy two copies of each book you think the children will like. Put them in with the rest of the library's books. If they just sit there, you don't need to get more of them. If they're immediately taken out, buy additional copies. My library, for example, has two copies of *Basketballs for Breakfast* and thirty-five copies of *Manchild in the Promised Land.*

If you decide to use structured reading levels, do not give students credit for books they read at home (assuming that some titles will be duplicated in the levels and the library) unless you've developed some system which takes that into account. Otherwise children will want credit for *Invisible Man* in two days, and the only way you can disprove them is by sharp questioning on the content. This usually leads to an otherwise avoidable scene.

The books below are listed in two parts. The first is those series which my students find so exciting that I can buy individual titles almost randomly. The second part is books that are not part of any series. The key is the same as before; * is hardcover, + is most popular, and × indicates books in which black or Puerto Rican characters play a predominant or significant role.

SERIES

PUBLISHER	SERIES TITLES
Berkley	Highland
Dell	Laurel Leaf
	Mayflower
	Yearling
Doubleday	Zenith
Fawcett-Crest	Beetle Baily

PUBLISHER	SERIES TITLES
	Dennis the Menace
	Peanuts
Grosset & Dunlap	Tempo
	Tell Me Why
Paperback Library	Dark Shadows
Platt & Munk	Fun-Time Activity Books
Pocket Books	Ripley's Believe It or Not
Preschool Press	Sesame Street
Pyramid	Mod Squad
Rand-McNally	Tip-Top Elf Books
Signet	Hawaii Five-O
	Laugh-In
	Mad
Washington Square Press	Archway
Western Publishing	Whitman Big-Little Books
	Whitman Big Tell-a-Tale Books
	Whitman Classics
	Whitman Tell-a-Tale Books
	Whitman TV Books
Wonder Books	How and Why

INDIVIDUAL TITLES

PUBLISHER	AUTHOR	TITLE
Ace	Raucher	+×*Watermelon Man*
	Weston	×*Heavyweight Champions*
Archway	Daly	+*Seventeenth Summer*
	Ish-Kishor	×*Joel Is the Youngest*
	Olds	×*Detour for Meg*
Avon	Mayerson	×*Two Blacks Apart*
Bantam	Bennett	×*Mister Fisherman*
	Fast	×*Freedom Road*

PUBLISHER	AUTHOR	TITLE
	Herndon	×*Way It Spozed to Be, The*
	Hunter	×*God Bless the Child*
	Steinbeck	*Of Mice and Men*
Berkley	Vroman	+×*Harlem Summer*
Cornerstone Library	Voege	+×*Beauty Secrets for Black Women*
Cowles*	Drotning	+×*Up from the Ghetto*
Crown*	Hughes and Meltzer	×*Pictorial History of the Negro in America, A*
Dell	Colman	×*Girl from Puerto Rico, The*
	Douglas	×*Hard to Tackle*
	Himes	×*Cotton Comes to Harlem*
	Lester	×*To Be a Slave*
	Moody	+×*Coming of Age in Mississippi*
	Richette	×*Throwaway Children, . The*
	Turner (ed.)	×*We, Too, Belong*
Dial	Brown	×*Die, Nigger, Die*
Doubleday*	Kipling	*New Illustrated Just So Stories*
Fawcett	Farr	×*Black Champion*
	Landers	+*Ann Landers Talks to Teen-Agers About Sex*
	Miller	×*Siege of Harlem, The*
	Pearce	*Cool Hand Luke*
	Robinson	×*Dark Companion: The Story of Matthew Henson*
Grosset & Dunlap*	Knight	*Lassie, Come Home*
Grove	Brown, Jr.	+×*Black Is*

PUBLISHER	AUTHOR	TITLE
	Lester	×*Look Out, Whitey! Black Power's Gon' Get Your Mama*
Harcourt, Brace*	Krementz	×*Sweet Pea*
	Young	×*Black Champions of the Gridiron*
Harper & Row*	Keats	×*Jennie's Hat*
		×*Little Drummer Boy, The*
	Silitoe	+×*Stevie*
	Stolz	×*Juan*
	White	*Trumpet of the Swan, The*
Hart	Neill	*Last Man Alive, The*
Houghton Mifflin*	Means	×*Canoe in the Mist*
Lancer	Holiday	×*Lady Sings the Blues*
	Teague	×*Letters to a Black Boy*
	Washington	×*Up from Slavery*
Lippincott	Archer	+×*Let's Face It*
Little, Brown*	Campanella	×*It's Good to Be Alive*
Macfadden-Bartell	Linn	×*Masque of Honor*
Macmillan*	Hamilton	×*Zeeley*
	Keats	×*Hi, Cat!*
Macrae*	Sullivan	×*Build, Brother, Build*
Noble	Russell	×*Go Up for Glory*
Paperback Library	Reynolds	*I, Willie Sutton*
Perennial	Decker	×*An Empty Spoon*
	Gibson	×*I Always Wanted to Be Somebody*
	King, Jr.	×*Stride Toward Freedom*

PUBLISHER	AUTHOR	TITLE
Pocket Books	Bristow	+×*Time for Glory*
	Shulman	×*West Side Story*
Popular Library	Gibson	×*From Ghetto to Glory*
	Kata	×*Patch of Blue, A*
Pyramid	Broudy	×*They Had a Dream*
	Hughes	×*An African Treasury*
Random House*	Angelou	×*I Know Why the Caged Bird Sings*
	Cohen	×*Color of Man, The*
	Reynolds	*F.B.I., The*
Scholastic Book Service	Arnothy	*I Am 15—and I Don't Want to Die*
	Neville	*It's Like This, Cat*
Signet	Cade (ed.)	×*Black Woman, The*
	Ford	×*Liberation of L. B. Jones, The*
	King, Jr.	×*Why We Can't Wait*
	Kohl	×*36 Children*
	Marine	×*Black Panthers, The*
	Styron	×*Confessions of Nat Turner, The*
Tempo	Lacy	×*Sleep in Thunder*
Viking*	Keats	×*Snowy Day, The*
Vintage	Carmichael	×*Black Power: The Politics of Liberation in America*
	Gorro	×*Block, The*
Westminster*	Berg	+×*What Harry Found When He Lost Archie*
	Blakey and Collver	×*Calypso Island*
	Cushman	×*Tom B. and the Joyful Noise*

PUBLISHER	AUTHOR	TITLE
	Emery	*Sky Is Falling, The*
	Summers	*You Can't Make It by Bus*
	Turner	×*Nipper*

MAGAZINES FOR THE URBAN CLASSROOM

It doesn't pay to subscribe to these magazines if you're on a nine- or ten-month school year. Instead, use the magazines to teach the kids a little "social discipline." Make one child in your class responsible for buying the latest copy of the magazine when it comes out (out of your money, not his). The "best" are marked +.

TITLE

Black Beauty
Black Pride
Black World (formerly *Negro Digest*)
Children's Digest
+ *Ebony*
Essence
+ *Golden Magazine for Children*
Jack and Jill
Jet
Life
Look
Miss Black America
+ *New Lady*
+ *Philly Talk* (local)
Sepia

+ *Soul Illustrated*
   Sports Illustrated
+ *Tan*

(Answer to "Stupid Stinky": 15 CENTS.)

APPENDIX:
STATISTICAL RESULTS

STUDENT REACTION TO GROUPED BASAL TEXT
READING VERSUS INDIVIDUALIZED READING
USING STRUCTURED LEVELS

I asked my students, as part of their annual evaluation of me and the way I conduct the class, to write down whether they "liked" or "hated" the way they did their reading.

During the year that I used grouped reading with basal texts, 52 percent of the children said they liked it, 48 percent said they didn't. Those who disliked it were characterized by such statements as "I hate the way our reading is like," "I hate that reading book."

The next year, when I used the individualized approach, 85 percent of the children said they enjoyed it, 15 percent did not. Those who didn't usually had quite singular reasons, not the least of which was that "sometimes it strains my eyes."

STATISTICAL RESULTS OF THE PROGRAM

During my second year—when I used the group method of teaching reading—I ran an informal pre- and post-test of my students. The results showed progress about 60 percent greater than could have been "expected" (see below). During my third year, I set up a much more formal and rigid (and audited) experiment to see whether my individualized approach would be measurably more successful.

In September, 1969, I gave each of my five classes the Stanford Reading Achievement Test (Intermediate Form X). My most academically advanced section, 8-1, scored 6.04. This score is two years below the national norms. (The national norms increase one academic month for each calendar month during the school year, so a student at the beginning of eighth grade should be reading at an 8.00 level.)

In May, nine months later, I gave my 8-1 class a post-test to see how much progress they had made during their year with me (Stanford, Intermediate Form W). If my program had had no effect on their reading ability, 8-1's score would have gone up from 6.04 to 6.72. This "expected gain" of about 7 months is based on the past performance of the students in 8-1. Over their past seven years in school they had a tendency to improve only 7 months in reading ability for every 9 months in school. Instead of going up from 6.04 to 6.72, however, the post-test showed that they had advanced to 7.41. This means that they had gained 7 months more than "expected," showing statistically a "Gain Over Expected Gain" of 101 percent. Also, 8-1's result of 7.41 indicated that they made progress at a rate 50 percent greater than the national norms. From September to May, the national norms advanced 9 months. 8-1's score advanced almost 14 months. In table form, the results read:

Class	No. Students	Pre Test (Stan. X) Sept. 1969	Ex-pected Gain To:	Post-Test (Stan. W) May 1970	Gain Over Ex-pected Gain	Gain Over National Norm
8-1	28	6.04	6.72	7.41	101%	50%

In the same way, my 8-2 class initially scored 5.06, or three years below the national norms (8.00). Their "expected gain," based on their past rate of progress, was 5.63. Instead, post-testing showed that they actually gained over 14 months, to 6.52. This increase is 9 months more than expected, or a "Gain Over Expected Gain" of 156 percent. In addition, this 14-month gain is an increase over the national norms of over 5 months, or 62 percent. In tabular form:

Class	No. Students	Pre-Test	Ex-pected Gain To:	Post-Test	Gain Over Ex-pected Gain	Gain Over National Norm
8-2	27	5.06	5.63	6.52	156%	62%

The table that follows shows the testing results for each of my five classes:

PROGRESS BY CLASS

Class	No. Students	Pre-Test	Expected Gain	Post-Test	Gain Over Gain	Gain Over Norm
8-1	28	6.04	6.72	7.41	101%	50%
8-2	27	5.06	5.63	6.52	156%	62%
8-7	22	4.22	4.69	5.18	104%	7%
8-9	28	3.80	4.23	4.99	177%	33%
8-13	22	3.17	3.53	4.12	164%	6%

The average of all 127 students shows an initial reading level of 4.53 in September, 1969. Their expected gain was 5 months, to 5.04. Instead, the average increased to 5.79. This is a gain over gain of 129.4 percent, and a gain over the rate of progress of the national norm of 30 percent:

Total No. Students	Pre-Test	Expected Gain	Post-Test	Gain Over Gain	Gain Over Norm
127	4.53	5.04	5.79	129.4%	30%

These numbered results take on a little more life when they're presented visually. What this bar graph shows (see page 171) is the number of students reading at each grade level in September, 1969, then again in May, 1970.

RESULTS OF MY PROGRAM

EXPLANATION: This graph shows the number of students reading at each grade level in September, 1969, and in May, 1970. September is in white, May is shaded. The total number of students is 127.

Grade level refers to a student's ability, not his actual grade in school. In September, for example, there were 28 eighth-graders who were reading on a third-grade level; in May, there were 11.

Some of the contrasts are rather striking. In September, for instance, there were 49 students reading at under a fourth-grade level; by May, there were only 16. At the other end of the graph, there were only 7 eighth-graders reading at or above a seventh-grade level at the start of the year; by the end of the year the 7 had become 28, including 2 students who were reading at a twelfth-grade level.

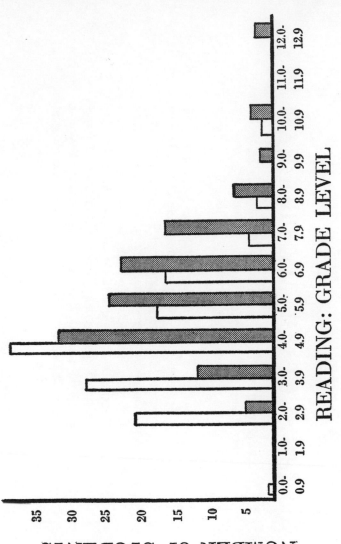

READING: GRADE LEVEL